# THE THAI VILLAGE ECONOMY IN THE PAST

## CHATTHIP NARTSUPHA

Original Thai Edition, 1984

เศรษฐกิจหมู่บ้านไทยในอดีต

Translated by

Chris Baker and Pasuk Phongpaichit

T0385018

Silkworm Books

ISBN: 978-974-7551-09-9

First edition published in 1999 by
Silkworm Books
430/58 M. 7, T. Mae Hia, Chiang Mai 50100, Thailand
P.O. Box 296, Phra Singh Post Office, Chiang Mai 50205
info@silkwormbooks.com
http://www.silkwormbooks.com.

Typeset in Garamond Premier Pro 11 pt. by Silk Type

Printed and bound in Thailand by O. S. Printing House, Bangkok

5  4  3  2

# CONTENTS

# AUTHOR'S PREFACE TO THE TRANSLATION

I'm very pleased that *The Thai Village Economy in the Past* is being published in English. I would like to express my thanks to Chris Baker and Pasuk Phongpaichit who have made a translation which conveys the meaning accurately and is also concise and readable. Also, they have written an afterword setting this book into the context of my research and thinking over many years. I consider this the most important book I have written and I feel very honoured that it has now been translated into English.

The research for this book changed me. From this point on, my academic work became completely focused on the village community. The work developed from the community economy to the community culture; from the Thai community in Thailand to the Tai communities outside Thailand; from historical time to contemporary time; from community in the locality to the community as a constituent part of the nation. Knowledge of and contact with the villagers made me shift my focus of study away from the economy and culture of the state and capitalism, towards the economy and culture of the villager and the village community. I changed my angle of vision away from state and capital and tried to adopt the angle of vision of the ordinary villager. The method of study changed too—from reading government documents and statistics about wealth, international trade, government finance, banking and so on, to interviewing ordinary people and listening to the accounts of their lives, difficulties, and struggles for subsistence. I take pride in the fact that I have attempted to recount the life history of the Thai people.

I hope that this work and my subsequent works have presented a picture which is not only realistic but also reflects the feelings, hopes, and dreams of the Thais. I have become part of what I study. I think that this work and my later works are in reality the outcome of the collective knowledge and research passed down by Thai villagers as a whole. I am just one descendant who has simply transferred their accounts onto paper and made them available to a wider audience.

Chatthip Nartsupha
9 April 1999

# TRANSLATORS' NOTE

The approach of this translation can be illustrated by the opening sentence. *Chon phao thai tham na pen lak* might be rendered as "The ethnic Thai peoples are principally rice-growers." However we have chosen the simpler "Thai peoples are rice-growers" on grounds that it conveys the meaning but also something of the directness and simplicity of the original's style and tone.

Similarly with the footnotes, the approach has been to provide all of the information in the original, but to adjust and simplify the presentation so that the result follows English-language academic conventions. References to publications have been brought into line with Chicago Documentation One. Archival references use the conventions of other English-language writers who have used these sources (especially Tej Bunnag). Citations of interviews have been changed from names to numbered references into the list of interviewees. This means that the numbering remains the same as in the Thai original (with the addition of a letter denoting region), while English-language users do not have to wrestle with Thai-language alphabetic order when trying to locate an entry in the list. The interview tapes are deposited in the National Library. References to Thai-language translations of English and French originals have been traced back to the original. Finally, the footnotes in chapter 5 have been renumbered to run throughout the chapter (in the original the renumbering restarted at section 5.2, while other chapters ran continuous).

We have added no explanatory notes. In a few places, denoted by square brackets, we have inserted some explanatory material in the text, such as the botanical names of plants which have no conventional English translation.

เศรษฐกิจหมู่บ้านไทยในอดีต

# THE THAI VILLAGE ECONOMY
# IN THE PAST

## CHATTHIP NARTSUPHA

# CONTENTS

For the village elders

whose collective memories have had no place in Thai history

# PREFACE

This research has been greatly helped by *achan* in teachers colleges and by local intellectuals, both in the academic respect and in the logistics of transport and lodging. They helped to select the villagers for interview, helped with interviewing, helped with interpretation of local language, and helped to analyse the data gathered each day. In addition, they took me to the villages, contacted and reassured the villagers, on many occasions provided me with accommodation at the teachers college and with transport, and allowed me to borrow research reports on village history by the college students. Without this help, I could not have done this research. Let me then express my utmost thanks to the teachers college *achan* and local intellectuals, especially Achan Udom Nipriyai, Nakhon Sithammarat Teachers College; Achan Sumali Wilairat, Chombung Teachers College; Achan Charik Bunchai, Thepsatri College; Achan Sutthada Lekwaithun, Ubon Ratchathani Teachers College; Achan Surat Warangkharat, Sakon Nakhon Teachers College; Achan Yongyot Lekklang, Ayutthaya Teachers College; Achan Chuklin Anuwichit, Chiang Rai Teachers College; Achan Pricha Uitrakun and Achan La-othong Amarinrat, Korat Teachers College; Achan Kitti Tanthai, Songkhla Teachers College; Achan Sangop Prasoetphan and Achan Chanphen Bangmek, Uttaradit Teachers College; Achan Yuphin Khemmuk, Chiang Mai Teachers College; Khun Pradit Siriratchataphong, Office of Education, Loei province; Khun Phenchai Sirorot, Wat U-mong, Chiang Mai; Khun Muanchon Suksaeng, Darin Bookshop, Phichit; together with the rectors, officers, teaching staff, and many students of the above-named teachers colleges who also helped with this research.

Thanks to four of my students who took part in the research and helped in many different ways through the six years of this project both academically and personally, including taking the risks of travelling into remote and dangerous areas, willingly letting me use their data cards and tapes and the research data they collected about the villages of each region and the Chinese. The four are Achan Pranut Sapphayasan, Mahasarakham Teachers College; Achan Chusit Chuchat, Chiang Mai Teachers College; Khun Suwit Phaithayawat, Sukhothai Thammathirat University; and Khun Sirilak Sakkriangkrai, Bank of Thailand. Thanks also to Khun Sakdina Chatkun na Ayutthaya, another student, who helped to locate pictures, documents, and books.

Dr Nithi Eosiwong, Dr Likhit Dhiravegin, Achan Chalatchai Ramitanon, Dr Prathip Nakhonchai, Achan Surasing Samruam Chimphanao, Achan Kanoksak Kaewthep, Khun Seksan Prasoetkun, and Khun Chanvit Chariyanukun read this work and made useful recommendations. Many thanks.

Achan Chirati Tingsaphat helped to translate materials from French about the mode of production in Laos. Many thanks.

Thanks to Chulalongkorn University which allowed me a sabbatical year to collect material (1982), and allowed me to travel upcountry to lecture and research many times as official duty.

In this research I used three archives, namely the Wachirayan Archive, the National Archives, and the Payap College Archive. Thanks to the staff of all three, especially to Khun Khanittha Wongphanit, Herbert Swanson, and Khun Waruni Osatharom for their good advice and assistance.

In the course of this research, I had the opportunity to carry out library research in Japan at the Centre for Southeast Asian Studies, Kyoto University in November 1979, and in the Netherlands at the Institute of Social Studies, The Hague, in April–May 1982. I would like to express my gratitude to both institutions, and to thank Professor Yasukichi

Yasuba at Kyoto University, and Professor Joost Kuitenbrouwer in The Hague for inviting me.

Lastly, to the highly respected village elders who were kind enough to be interviewed, I cannot thank you enough for the utmost assistance, trust, and sympathy you afforded me, even though many of you were not in good health. Further, let me state that this work has been written by you as well, and let me express my wish that I can stand with you and your descendants in the struggle over the culture of Thai society all my life.

Chatthip Nartsupha
Samsen Nai, Bangkok
25 March 1984

# CHAPTER ONE

# FROM THE PRIMORDIAL VILLAGE COMMUNITY TO THE VILLAGE UNDER THE SAKDINA SYSTEM

THAI peoples are rice-growers.[1] In early times, they grew rice on high ground but later gradually moved more and more to the valleys. In the north of Thailand and in the mountainous Shan States, Thais planted rice in the valleys between the hills.[2] Thai communities in Sipsongpanna, southern China, and Ahom communities in Assam, India, planted rice in the valleys in the same way, that is, along the banks of the Mekong river in Sipsongpanna and the Dawpi (Brahmaputra) river in Assam.[3] The Chiang Rung chronicles record: "wherever there is water, there are the Thai".[4] This fact was confirmed by Dr Dodd who travelled through southern China in 1910, making a survey of Thai peoples. In his book, Dodd wrote: "Wherever there is water for their rice fields the Tai live. They do not live in the mountains."[5] Jit Phumisak summed up very appropriately that one of the common elements of the culture of Thai peoples is "cultivating paddy in low land".[6]

On the hill slope above lived various hill peoples or old local communities who grew dry rice and vegetables,[7] or collected from the forest food[8] and other products such as cotton, rattan, lac, and fruit which they exchanged for rice and cloth with the Thai on the plains.[9] These peoples did not stay permanently in one place and practised shifting cultivation.[10] Their level of existence was lower than the Thai peoples who established settlements and practised agriculture. Among these local peoples were the Lua, Khamu, and Thin in the north, Kha, Kui and Suai in the northeast, and the Ngo Sakai in the south.[11] While the Thai communities in the lowlands developed to the level of state formation, these local peoples were not able to form states of their own.[12]

The economic and social structure of the old Thai communities took the form of a primordial community. The village owned the land in common. Robert Lingat quoted a French academic that in the Thai communities of Tongkin, the land was periodically redistributed among members of the village by the village head. If someone moved away from the village, the land was returned to the village.[13] Traces of this practice of periodic redistribution survived in later periods, for instance in the region of Hua Phan in Laos.[14] But rights were limited; if a piece of land lay unused for a certain period, such as three or four years, the land reverted to the community. Research by Georges Condominas[15] and Shigeharu Tanabe confirms this. From his study of Thai Lue communities in Sipsongpanna, Tanabe concluded that land ownership was vested jointly in the village community and that land was periodically redistributed to maintain equality among members of the village community, in a fashion similar to that found among the Tai communities in Tongkin.[16]

The kind of self-government found in these primordial Tai communities can still be traced in the system of councils of village elders found in some northeastern villages. In Nawa Tai village, Phosai, Ubon Ratchathani, if a dispute arises over family affairs, courtship, or livelihood, it is treated as a quarrel among members of a single family. Each party to the dispute nominates four or five elders to a council which debates the issue and makes a ruling—perhaps demanding an apology or a fine, and reprimanding those involved not to continue the misbehaviour. This council of elders system still exists in Nawa Tai village down to this day.[17] Self-rule is the ideal of villagers. It is a blessing from the past which villagers long to retain. The desire for self-rule regularly surfaces during peasant revolts. Villagers always want to create a village free from the power of the state.[18]

Later the Thai primordial village developed into the sakdina system. There appeared a state or king at the head of a larger community which dominated over many village communities. Condominas, who studied the political system of Tai-Dai speaking peoples, concluded that in areas where a state (king) appeared and established ownership over all the land, the king shared out the land under the control of the nobles and denied land ownership to individuals.[19] Stone inscriptions, the Three Seals law, and contemporary writings by foreign travellers provide evidence for this state of affairs during the Sukhothai and Ayutthaya periods.[20] But even before the Sukhothai and Ayutthaya periods, the Asian sakdina system with no private property rights had already appeared in the Thai communities. On the basis of studies by Bishop Burnay, Lingat suggested that villagers in the Luang Prabang region had no knowledge of private property right. Land belonged to the "lord of life", the king of Luang Prabang. Ordinary people had only the usage right to collect things from the land or work on the land. The land tax which villagers paid each year took the form of a rental from the king.[21] The same held true among the Thai-Ahom. The king was the sole landowner. He divided the land among the nobles according to their official positions, and the nobles held the land only as long as they held their office.[22] In the society of Sipsongpanna, some of the land was given into the control of nobles as part of their official position and retained only as long as the noble held the position.[23] Similarly in the Thai Yai communities in the Shan States, each lord was owner of all the land in his state.[24] In the Lanna kingdom, the Law of Mengrai stated clearly: "the whole land belongs to the king".[25] The implication is as follows. During the Sukhothai and Ayutthaya periods, Thai society under the influence of Khmer culture and Buddhism crystallised into the sakdina system marked by stronger government. Yet even before this, ancient Thai society had already developed into the sakdina system of its own accord. A larger community, headed by the state or king, claimed ownership of all the land, over the head of the smaller community, the village. Thus no system of private ownership of land emerged either in ancient Thai society or in the society of Thai sakdina.

In Sukhothai and Ayutthaya society, the state clearly claimed to own all land. Yuk Sriariya has drawn attention to the important thesis on Thai economic history by Vithit Sajjapong (A preliminary study on economic history of premodern Thailand) which proposed for the first time that land in the Sukhothai kingdom belonged to the king.[26] Vithit's source was Inscription 49 which shows that when land was presented to a *wat*, the occupant of the land had first to request the land from the king.[27] As for the Ayutthaya period, the Miscellaneous Laws (*phra aiyakan bet set*) clause 52 laid down explicitly that "land in the territory of Ayutthaya is the land of the king. If it is given to people who are subjects of the realm, it cannot be their property."[28] And clause 54 of the same laws laid down that "land which is outside the territory of the royal capital of Ayutthaya does not belong to the people either. Buying and selling is prohibited."[29] Moreover, for individuals even the right to occupy land was not secure. The old royal law clause 44 laid down that rice land which the occupant had left unused for only one year was considered as abandoned.[30] Clause 65 of the Miscellaneous Laws stated that the occupant of land left unused for over three years lost the occupancy right completely.[31] Nicolas Gervaise, a foreign visitor to Ayutthaya, stated that land belonged to the state.[32] Lingat summed up that the land law in Ayutthaya had three main principles:[33] first, the king was the owner of the land of the kingdom; second, ordinary people could not buy and sell land; third, peoples' rights over land were very weak because they were tied to occupancy; if land was left idle and someone else came to cultivate it, the previous occupant lost any rights immediately. The state's claim to own all the land emerged clearly as a system in 1455 when King Trailokanat promulgated the law to distribute land under the sakdina system to various official positions according to rank.[34] This system remained in force for the 416 years of the Ayutthaya period.

In the Rattanakosin period before the Fourth Reign, the land system of the Ayutthaya period remained in use. The Three Seals law was revised in the First Reign for use in the Rattanakosin period. When John Crawfurd arrived in 1823, he wrote that: "the land . . . is considered the property of the king".[35] It was only in 1861 under the Fourth Reign, that a royal edict was promulgated stating that if the king wanted land which was currently occupied, he must pay full compensation to the occupant.[36] Yet private property rights were not yet guaranteed with any certainty.

The 1891 government proclamation concerning railways still stated that "all the land in the kingdom belongs to the king".[37] Prince Dilok Nopparat, a son of King Chulalongkorn, wrote in a thesis in 1907 that "the land in all parts of the country belongs to the government, and the occupants have only the right of usage".[38] Even after the 1932 reforms, in the meeting of the special commission on the national economic plan (March 1933), M.C. Sakon Wannakon Worawan and Luang Pradit Manutham both agreed that Siam in the past had upheld the principle that all land belonged to the king or the state.[39] Lingat believes that clear acceptance of private property rights came after the 1932 reform, when the state passed an act about forcible acquisition of property (1934). From this point onwards, there was no claim that land belonged to king or state. Lingat wrote: "After this act came into use, we can conclude that the old legal principle that the king owned all the land in the kingdom ceased to provide the basis for forcible purchase."[40]

However, the imposition of the rule of the city and the state over the village community did not destroy the village community. The state merely claimed the right of land ownership, superseding the claim of the village community, in order to legitimate the state's demand for corvée and tax. The community remained coherent and solid internally with respect to relations with land, cooperation in various activities, and spiritual expression (on which see below).

Yet the development of the sakdina system forced the villages which previously had grown rice for subsistence use in the village only, to produce also for the state's tolls. Exploitation arose. In the Ayutthaya period, male villagers in the prime of life had to work as corvée labour for six months in the year. In the Rattanakosin period, this was reduced to four months (1785, in the First Reign) and then three months (1810, in the Second Reign).[41] Besides the labour tax there were also produce taxes levied on rice and forest goods.[42] After the power of Vientiane had been destroyed in 1828 under the Third Reign, Isan villages had to send produce taxes to Bangkok.[43] Lanna villages were drafted directly under the power of the Bangkok state in the Fifth Reign.[44]

The crystallisation of the sakdina system among the Thai communities during the Ayutthaya period—shown most clearly in King Trailokanat's promulgation of the sakdina law in 1455—ran in parallel with the spread of Hinayana Buddhism, which had originally been introduced 700 years ago. After villages had come under the power of the state, they also began to come under the ideology of Buddhism. The spread of Buddhism from the centre amounted to a direct historical assault on the local spirits of village and town. This assault can still be seen in the spirit medium ritual in the north in the present day. In tambon Mae Hia, on the slope of Doi Suthep, Chiang Mai, rituals reflect conflict between the Buddhism of the rulers and the local spirits from ancient times. In one spirit medium ceremony, grandfather and grandmother Sae contest with Buddha, using supernatural power to expand their physical size in the fight. They ultimately lose and must accept the superiority of the Buddha. They agree to share a portion of the sacred offerings with the Buddha, and to stop sacrificing humans, but to sacrifice cows or bullocks instead.[45] However, similar to the survival of the village subsistence economy, the belief in local spirits survived under the umbrella of Buddhism whose main purpose at the state level was to confirm the legitimacy of the king (on which see more below).

The domination of the sakdina system over the village was only external domination. The sakdina state periodically extracted labour services and taxes, and spread the Buddhist ideological beliefs about merit and Buddhist ceremonies. But under the sakdina system, land was not divided among the sakdina nobles as owners. There were no landowners in the countryside like the lords of the manor in Europe who managed the cultivation on the land under their responsibility. The intervention of the sakdina system or the sakdina class in village production was very limited. The village only had to pay taxes of rice, forest produce, and labour services. These periodic levies satisfied the state. In later times, some villages did not have to deliver corvée labour, but paid in produce or money instead. Bishop Pallegoix stated that these villagers (*phrai suai*) were probably the happiest because they did not have to work on behalf of the king.[46] Farmers under the sakdina system did not have to deal with landowners as under the feudal system.[47] This had the effect of allowing the village production system to fall into a backward and undeveloped state, remaining unchanged from the era of the primordial village. The sakdina system only exerted domination over the primordial village community in order to extract the surplus in the form of labour and goods. The productive capacity of the village probably scarcely increased throughout the sakdina period, and a system of private property in land developed very slowly and incompletely.

# CHAPTER TWO

# THE SUBSISTENCE VILLAGE ECONOMY UNDER THE SAKDINA SYSTEM, 1455–1855

## 2.1 Production

Village production under the sakdina system was subsistence production, meaning production for own use and not for sale or exchange.[1] Villagers have the phrase *ha kin* "seeking to eat"[2] or *ha yu ha kin* "seeking to live and eat";[3] the implication is that villagers are satisfied if they have food.[4] When they are not busy, village males will ask one another, "tomorrow shall we go look for wild animals to eat," while females talk about weaving[5] or going in search of food.[6] In both cases, the subject is seeking food for subsistence. Many elders paint a clear picture of the subsistence production in past times: "for eating, not for selling";[7] "for food, don't know where to sell";[8] or "cannot just idle about, must seek to eat and live".[9] The official records and writings from the Fifth Reign reflect the image of a village subsistence economy. For instance, it is stated "people buy and sell only a very little"[10] or "products which are made are rarely sold".[11] One villager described this state of affairs with the words "in the beginning things had no price".[12]

The most important subsistence activity of the village was growing rice. It was much more important than other forms of production. Village rice-growing under the sakdina system was directed mainly to consumption within the family household.

Rice production was very backward, relying mainly on labour, animals, rain-water, plough, hoe, and rake. Rice cultivation began with clearing the forest using human labour. When the rains came, farmers started ploughing in May (around the sixth month of the waning moon, or the seventh if the rains came late). At first they sowed broadcast. Once they had made bunds to hold water in the fields, they changed from broadcast to transplanting[13] as the yield per *rai* was higher. At the very beginning when they had no ploughs, they would chase a buffalo herd round the fields to trample the earth. This was known as *wian khwai*, the buffalo round. On plots of twenty to thirty *rai*, the trampling took around ten days. In that period, they still did not know how to use a plough. One elder in tambon Mai Fat, amphoe Sikao, Trang province had seen a buffalo herd used for trampling because nobody yet had a plough to use.[14] At tambon Mai Fat, the plough came into use only in 1903.[15] In fields on high ground or hill slopes, villagers planted dry rice or practised swiddening. In these narrow fields, a plough or buffalo could not be used. They used a hoe to clear the grass, and then made holes with a stick for the rice seed. The practice was called *suk khao*, dibbling rice.[16] Once they moved to the valley, they used a plough but still used a hoe to break up the earth ahead of the plough and rake.[17] The first ploughs were wholly wooden, without even a metal tip. With later development, they strapped an iron tip onto the wooden plough at the point where the plough broke the earth.[18] Later still, the metal tip was fitted over the wood. Seventy years ago, old-style wooden ploughs with iron tips strapped on could still be seen, for example in amphoe Ranot, Songkhla province.[19]

Once the rice was planted, the major factor was the supply of water. Farmers depended totally on rain-water as Thai sakdina society had no irrigation systems except in the north where farmers of many villages joined together to create the system of *muang* (water-delivery canals) and *fai* (weirs to dam streams). Farmers along the banks of the rivers were somewhat better off as they could rely on the river water, known as *nam tha* (water on the spot). This was one reason why many settlements were sited along the river banks. Other farmers had to depend on the rain alone, and some could collect the water using bunds around their fields.[20] As Prince Damrong wrote about the paddy fields in the central plain: "Monthon Phayap [i.e. northern] farmers know how to irrigate. But since ancient times the people in the interior *monthon* [old territorial division larger than province] such as Ayutthaya and Bangkok have only ever cultivated with rain-water and river water."[21] In Isan, in Korat province during the Fifth Reign, 90 percent used rain-water and only 10 percent used water from streams.[22]

Because Thai rice farmers had to depend on rain-water (or as the Sipsongpanna people call it, *na nam fa*, sky-water ricefields),[23] the yield was not regular. Every one year in three on average, water would be deficient, while once in a while there would be a major flood. From statistics kept in Ayutthaya province for 123 years (1829–1953), there was severe drought in thirty-nine years and heavy flooding in four.[24] Thai farmers in the past had no technology high enough to overcome this fact of nature. They had to depend on fate and fortune to get natural rainfall of just the right amount. But very often they had to face a situation of *fon laeng nam lang* (a drought or a bath),[25] meaning that rain either did not fall or fell so much it flooded and the fields were ruined. Both cases happened over centuries. In addition, farmers had no knowledge of fertiliser, except for the droppings of work animals and minerals brought down by flood waters.[26] The yield per *rai* was hence static over a long time.[27] Thus the major problems of farmers were that they grew only rice, depended on the rain, had no irrigation, and were in a bad state if the rains failed. If they could not grow rice in one year, they had to go without food or borrow for up to three years. If the drought continued, then the debt was like "earth piling up on a pig's tail"—it accumulated.[28] The importance of rain for the life of the farmer was clearly reflected in old complaints such as *fon mai mi phuak rao cha yae*, "no rain, we are lost";[29] and *b'mi nam tham na nai pi fon laeng*, "no water for rice in a drought year".[30] In any year that the rice crop was good, they would be very happy. As the father of one interviewee said: *sabai laeo khrao ni thung pi na mai dai tham na ko mai pen rai*, "so happy now that I don't care if I cannot grow rice next year".[31]

When the rainfall was right, the crop would be good. It would be ripe enough to harvest from around November to February. The timing differed according to location and crop strain. Early rice (*khao bao*) was usually harvested in December, heavy rice (*khao nak*) in February.[32] Harvesting again used mainly human labour. The tool was a sickle, except in the south where a *kae* (harvest) knife was used to cut handfuls known as *liang*—gathering only the ear not the stalk as with the sickle.[33] At harvest time in the central region, the water may not have completely disappeared. Farmers might have to use a punt boat to reach the fields where the paddy was ripe, and step down into the water to harvest. In the evening, they would go back to pick up the piles of harvested paddy, transport them by boat back to the house, and pile them up in the yard. If the water had dried, then they could transport by sled. During the harvest, they might have to work at night also.[34] The harvested paddy was threshed by buffalo or people trampling the stalks to separate the grains from the ears, and then winnowed by throwing the seeds into the air and catching them in a basket, letting the chaff and dust be blown away by the wind. The remaining unhusked paddy would be stored in the rice barn. When needed to eat, it would be brought and pounded in a mortar each day.

Apart from rice, another major food of the Thais in all regions was fish.[35] Fish were caught using several simple methods including scoops, spears,[36] traps set along the river edge and lit with a flame torch at night,[37] holes dug in the dried-up river bed,[38] dams built across canals during the dry season,[39] baited traps which small fishes could enter but not exit,[40] nets set across the current,[41] and hooks. In the south, there was a method so easy it is scarcely believable. It was called the ghost boat. A whitewashed plank was attached to the side of the boat down to the level of the boat's bottom; the boat was paddled to the edge of a stream overgrown with weeds; fish which are easily frightened like mullet and bass would leap up in panic and fall in the boat.[42] Because in the past fish were so plentiful, with simple methods such as these villagers could catch fish with little difficulty. These fishing methods used simple tools or almost no tools at all, mostly labour. Similarly fish were caught all along the coastline without going far out to sea. At first the boats were dugouts which held one or two people, were propelled by paddle or sail, and could not venture far from the coast.[43] To illustrate how plentiful fish were, villagers said they would boil the rice and pound the curry paste before going out to fish,[44] or even simply catch fish by hand.[45] In the central region, snakehead fish (*pla chon*) and soft-flesh fish (*pla nua on*) were the easiest to catch.[46] They were used to make dried fish and salted fish, or fermented fish in the northeast.[47] The areas with the most fish were valleys which flooded for a long time or big lakes. Examples of such big lakes were found to the west of the Chaophraya river in amphoe Phak Hai, Ayutthaya; in amphoe Bang Plama, Suphanburi; Lake Siphai; various ponds in Phichit; Lake Boraphet in Nakhon Sawan; the Songkhram river valley in Sakon Nakhon and Nakhon Phanom; along the banks of the Mekong river; and along the coastline in the south. In the central region, besides fish there were prawns in profusion. They could be caught underwater just by hand where they clustered around house pillars.[48] In the south shellfish were dug up using a sharp stick,[49] and crabs were caught by using a dip net or by laying a string and waiting to pull it up when the crab grabbed the string with its claws.[50]

Villagers who lived close to the forest could seek extra food by hunting animals such as wild cows, wild buffaloes, wild boar, deer, barking deer, and wild hens.[51] A Kha interviewee at Dong Luang, Nakhon Phanom said that in olden times when animals were plentiful, there was no need to plant crops.[52] The weapons used ranged from bow-and-arrow used in the past, through flintlock guns, to percussion-cap guns in later times.[53] Sometimes nets were used.[54] In Isan, people also ate small animals such as squirrels, lizards, and monitor lizards. Groups would regularly go out in the afternoon to find these animals, calling it *pai ha kap khao* (finding food to go with the rice).[55] Farmers would find vegetables on the *pluak na*, hummocks along the bunds of the rice fields. When the area was being cleared for planting, big tree stumps would be left in place, because the farmers did not have enough strength to dig them out. Each year they would dig out some more. After the rains, these hummocks would sprout edible shoots, *tamlung* [*Melothria heterophylla*], *liang* [a vegetable] and fungi which the villagers collected to eat.[56] At the edges of the fields, morning glory would appear naturally.[57] These vegetables could also be collected from the forest.[58] Especially in the north, where the plains lie at the foot of the mountains, villages close to the hills and forests could collect roots, fungi, and bamboo shoots. Sometimes farmers also planted vegetables such as beans of various types, eggplant, sesame, chilli, muskmelon, water-melon, and maize. Around their houses, villagers planted big fruit trees such as mango and rose-apple, and kitchen vegetables such as onions, ginger, galangal, and lemongrass.[59]

Villagers wove their own cloth. They used ordinary looms, planted their own cotton, and raised their own silkworms. Cotton could only be grown on high ground. Many villages did not have enough suitable land for growing cotton, so they had to buy or barter. The ripe cotton bolls were pounded into the form of cotton wool, spun with a wheel into yarn, and then woven into cloth. Even in the central region which is a low-lying area, many places made yarn from cotton they grew themselves. For instance in amphoe Tha Rua, Ayutthaya province, yarn was still made locally at the end of the nineteenth century. Cotton was grown in Phichit and Phitsanulok provinces, and in the upper part of amphoe Pak Phanang and amphoe Lan Saka of Nakhon Sithammarat province in the south. In Isan, cotton was widespread in Ubon Ratchathani, Kalasin, Mahasarakham, Nakhon Phanom, and Loei provinces.[60] In old Thai society, weaving for own use was widespread in all regions, including the central region.[61] Cloth from Khlong Takhian near the city of Ayutthaya was very famous even in Rattanakosin times.[62] Weaving was a female duty, undertaken mostly in the dry season, or in the rainy season after the field work was complete, such as when waiting for the rice to grow.[63] Spinning was done at night, especially moonlit nights, in what was known as *long khuang*, working in a special area, usually under the house.[64] It was a custom for young males to visit young girls in the space under the house during this time. This custom was widespread in Tai-Lao society in the past. Weaving cloth by loom was an important activity for the family and village, so that according to Tai-Lao custom, a girl who could not weave could not get married.[65] But weaving had no technological development. It used only human labour. Weaving a single *phanung* took two to three full days. It is important to note that households did both weaving and farming. Farming households were also weaving households. There was no distinct division of labour such that this person was a weaver and that person was a farmer. Weaving was not confined to separate weaving villages which did no paddy farming. Farming households in the past also wove, except in some very backward communities such as the Kha and Thin, who could not weave cloth and who had to barter raw cotton for cloth.[66]

Apart from the basics of food and cloth, villagers were subsistent in daily life in others ways. For building houses, they cut their own timber from the forest. Bamboo was especially important,[67] not only in building, but also for weaving into baskets for various purposes. After work in the fields, villagers made various production tools including nets, baskets (for carrying, storing rice, winnowing), hampers, carrying poles, chests for storing cloth, betelnut boxes, various fish traps,[68] even dug-out boats, and medium-sized canoes.[69] Firewood for cooking could be found easily from the forest.[70] To light a fire, at first they rubbed sticks to create a spark. Later they used stone and metal, and blew the flames to ignite small branches. Later still they used sap or latex mixed with wood scraps to make a bar known as a *krabong* (baton) which would burn for a long time, and was used to provide light at night.[71]

Farmers had a high level of subsistence. They could produce their own food, make their own cloth, and gather from nature such things as fish, vegetables, and timber. Usually villagers did not lack food but in years of drought or flood they might have no rice for that year. They would survive by borrowing rice from villages which did have a crop, or by gathering forest produce to exchange. At worst they could gather *kloi* from the forest. These root vegetable were similar to yams. They had to be soaked in water for five to six days, then dried in the sun, and steamed to eat with rice.[72]

In past times, those who were worst off were the indigenous peoples who lived in the deep forest or in the hills. They practised shifting cultivation, and had barely enough for subsistence. If they could not hunt animals, they lived off rice with salt and vegetables.[73] They often planted cotton to exchange for cloth with the farmers in the valleys.[74] In

Nan province the Lawa were so poor that a whole family had only one piece of cloth.[75]

Another occupation of farmers was gathering forest produce besides the animals and vegetables which they gathered for their own food. This was done mostly in the dry rather than wet season. This occupation gave the farmers a surplus above subsistence, but often a surplus which had to be handed over to the state as tax. In particular, villagers outside the central region who were far from the court often did not have to render corvée but had to send produce taxes instead. After the rice season was over, villages in Isan and the south often had no surplus of rice available for tax. So the state fixed the tax in forest produce such as hides, jute, cotton, birds nest, silk, cardamom, honey, ivory, gold, silver, tin, gems, copper, sulphur, sapan wood, teak, beeswax, wild cardamom, sandal wood, *marit* wood [*Diospyrus discolor*], *krak-khi* [*Cudrania javanensis*, a dye], *krak-khanun* [dye from jackfruit wood], *chaluk* [*Alyxia lucida*], rattan, *sato* [*Parkia speciosa*], *luk niang* [*Pithecolobium jiringa*], herbs, wild animals, and so on.[76]

The state kept a portion of these forest goods, and sold another portion as export. The *khlang* (finance) ministry managed this trade as a monopoly of the state or king. These products figured significantly in the list of products exported from Siam in the period before the Bowring treaty of 1855. For example, the Crawfurd papers dating from the Second Reign stated that Siam's exports included pepper, sapan wood, aloe wood, hides, rhino horn, deer antler, lac, and sugar. The major export destination was China.[77] At the end of the 1820s, Siamese exports also went to Penang, Malacca, and Singapore. The value of rice was only 14.7 percent of total exports.[78] At the start of the Fourth Reign (1852), Siam's major exports were sugar, hides, raw cotton, sapan wood, tin, lac, and various other forest goods. Rice ranked tenth and was not yet an important export product.[79] In his study of overseas trade and the internal economy in the thirty-five years before the Bowring treaty (1820–55), Ammar Siamwalla concluded that foreign trade had very little impact on the life of most Siamese, or on the working of the economy.[80] He states at one point: "The oddity in the case of Siam was that this independent co-existence between the export sector and the subsistence sector...existed here prior to [the] intrusion [of capitalism]."[81] Ammar's observation is correct. He also points out an important aspect of the Siamese economy revealed by the export statistics; in the period before the Bowring treaty of 1855 opened up the country for trade, the export economy of sakdina Siam was dominated by the trade in forest products. (In certain periods there were also some specialised exports from limited areas such as pepper and sugar).[82] Under the sakdina system, the collection of forest produce took the form of tax not trade, and exports were still under the tight monopolistic control of the finance ministry. Hence even though sale of forest produce in overseas markets was quite dynamic, the impact on production and trade of forest produce inside the country was very limited. The production of forest products was a supplementary form of production for tax. It was not the principal form of production. The basis of the internal production was subsistence. Throughout the sakdina period, the Siamese economy had a twin production system: subsistence production for internal use and forest products for export. As a result, the export of forest products did not break down the system of subsistence production.

The basic factors of production of the Thai subsistence economy were labour and natural resources, especially land. Because the level of production technology was low, human labour was the most important factor of production of the village under the sakdina system. Gathering food from nature, cultivating rice, weaving cloth, and collecting forest produce—all used labour as the factor of production. As already noted, tools and implements used in production were simple hand implements with no mechanisation. What division of labour there was in the village was based on the heaviness of each task and the strength of each individual rather than on any expertise gained from practice or study. Hence the division of labour tended to follow gender and age. Men hunted, fished, built houses, worked wood, made posts, sawed wood, made baskets, plaited rope, and carved wood; females wove cloth, dyed cloth, sewed, fetched water, husked rice, picked vegetables, and cooked. Both males and females worked in paddy farming but work was shared out with males ploughing and raking, women plucking and transplanting. Children looked after buffaloes and fetched water.[83] The importance of labour in production is reflected in the Isan villagers' traditional blessing: *yu di mi haeng* (*raeng*), stay well and have strength.[84] This strength or labour power was the basis of production in Thai society before the entry of the capitalist system. And labour power was household labour or surplus labour exchanged among households, not paid labour. This factor of production was present in sufficient supply in each village. This was the original basis of the Thai villagers' subsistence economy.

The maintenance of the subsistence production of the Thai village also depended on the availability of surplus resources, especially land. The ratio of land to population was higher in Siam than in neighbouring countries. Sir John Bowring estimated that in 1850 Siam had between 4.5 and 5 million people.[85] Prince Dilok Nopparat estimated that in 1904 Siam had 7 million people living in a total area of 634,000 square kilometres, or 11 persons per square kilometre.[86] In comparison, the density was 16 in Burma, 21 in Indonesia (including all islands), 25 in Philippines, and 73 in India.[87] In the same period. Prince Dilok Nopparat estimated that roughly 3 million out of this total lived in the central region or Lower Siam, 2 million in the south, and another 2 million in the north and northeast combined or Upper Siam. Even those in the central region did not feel crowded. They could still enlarge their cultivated area without difficulty by clearing more forest. Only the central region had villages of large size. In other regions, the villages were small and there were many isolated homesteads.[88] In Isan, statistics from 1896 state that on average villages in the Korat area had only 38 houses or 203 people.[89] The gradual extension of cultivated area made it possible to produce enough rice for consumption even with population increase. Elders in the central region can still remember that during their childhood at the start of this century, land was available in abundance. If anyone gave their children a lot of paddy land, the children might not like it because they would have to pay high tax for the occupancy. At first there were no disputed claims or quarrels. When *chanot* land ownership titles began to be issued towards the end of the Fifth Reign (1901), farmers refused to take up titles themselves. Sometimes they arranged for relatives and friends to join together and place many plots of land under a single name. Land was not yet in short supply and did not have much of a price.[90] Other regions were the same.[91] In the south, people who were forcibly moved from Saiburi [Kedah] to Nakhon Sithammarat province during the Second Reign, were given plots of land for cultivation, but went out at night and moved the boundary markers to reduce the area.[92]

Village subsistence production was dependent on nature. Villagers found food directly from nature or grew rice dependent on rainfall. They used human labour with no mechanical assistance. They carried out important crafts such as weaving in almost every village. They were highly self-reliant and could maintain this condition because of the surplus availability of natural resources in comparison to the number of people.

## 2.2 Relations of production

The basic relations of production of the village under the sakdina system had two dimensions. First, the village was a community which still had strong internal bonds, similar to the time of the primordial village. Second, the village was exploited from outside—by the state which had by now come into existence.

The internal bonds were based on the system of landholding linked to membership of the village community, mutual cooperation between members of the village, and kin or quasi-kin relations of village members. The strong internal bonds meant that the village could maintain its autonomy and its identity over a long period, even after the state had come into existence.

In the village's development from ancient times, the custom of periodically redistributing land disappeared. However, occupancy of land for cultivation was still linked to membership in the village. A family had to belong to the village in order to have land. This emerges clearly from historical study of the foundation and expansion of villages, especially in Isan. When a hunter or villager out travelling found a new area of fertile land, for instance in a valley with a pond, known in Isan language as *thi din dam nam chum* (dark earth with plentiful water),[93] he would invite relatives or friends from his old village to move their households to settle at the new site. Those who went to claim land at the new place became members of the group which established the new village,[94] and the right to claim land was confined to members of this group. As long as there was no widespread buying and selling of land, occupancy of land was passed down by inheritance within the families which were the units of the village community. So individuals did not occupy land directly but through their membership in the village which in reality controlled the land in that area. Hence the village community was highly important for the individual villagers. Individuals were tightly bound to the community, even though the community no longer claimed to control the land in common as clearly as in the period of the primordial village.

Apart from the new villages which arose when an old village became crowded and a group separated off to find new land to cultivate, some villages were forcibly created by the state as a result of people-raiding and forced resettlement after wars. Even communities created in this way maintained their internal bonds and acted as a community unit. The difference from other villages lay only in the forcible relocation. The state did not come in to manage the community internally any more than in the case of villages which were settled naturally. It even appears that in villages which were created from people-raiding or forcible resettlement after war, the internal bonds at the new location were even stronger than in villages settled because of natural expansion from an older community. Examples include the Mon villages at Phrapradaeng, Pakkret, Sam Khok, Ratchaburi, Samut Sakhon, Phetchaburi, Kanchanaburi, Uthai Thani, Ayutthaya, Singburi, Korat, and Lopburi; the Lao Phuan communities in Phichit, Suphanburi, Saraburi, Singburi, Lopburi, Sukhothai, Phrae, Uthai Thani, Kampaengphet, Phetchabun, and elsewhere; the Lao Song communities at Ratchaburi, Suphanburi, and elsewhere; the Phu Tai in Sakon Nakhon, Kalasin, Nakhon Phanom, and elsewhere; the Khmer in Suphanburi; and Saiburi Muslim communities in Nakhon Sithammarat.[95]

Mutual cooperation between members of the village was a very clear expression of the relations of production of the Thai village community. This cooperation was another factor binding individuals to the community. Mutual cooperation was seen in paddy farming, in cooperative labour for transplanting, harvest and threshing, known as *long khaek* (bringing a guest), *kan ao mu* (bringing a hand) or *so raeng*. In places where rice was transplanted, villagers helped one another to hoe earth to build bunds for holding water in the field—a practice known as *yok na* (raising the paddy field); in places where paddy was broadcast, they cooperated to build paths which allowed passage for man and buffalo and also provided grass to feed the buffalo. They also helped one another in winnowing, pounding, or polishing the rice by hand. Sometimes they brought their own tools such as buffalo, plough, rake, saw, and axe. The working principle was that whoever had finished his own work went to help those not yet finished.[96] Cooperative labour was also used in other activities, such as fishing in the south where setting a sein net across a stream required up to forty people. They called on others to contribute their manpower, and shared out the fish as reward.[97] Similarly in clearing the forest to make a fruit orchard, they called up manpower and axes.[98] In villages which had craft activities which needed to use a lot of labour at one time, labour was called up in the same way. For instance, beating metal to make knives and sickles needed four sturdy men working together. The product was shared.[99] In villages which got some of their livelihood from hunting, villagers joined together to go on a hunt. Even when hunting for small animals in the forest, they went together in numbers because they feared tigers.[100] To catch fish, several people cooperated to build dikes blocking the stream by driving in bamboos and tying them together with vines. Those who took part became joint owners of the pond behind the dike, and when the water fell they caught and shared the fish. In Isan, for instance, this practice known as *kat* was found in amphoe Sisongkhram, Nakhon Phanom.[101]

For long-distance trading, villagers teamed up to travel in groups of five to twenty people at a time. The *nai hoi* who drove cattle and buffaloes down from Isan to the central region worked this way.[102] This mutual cooperation among villagers extended to sharing rice to eat. During a time of scarcity, villagers might ask to borrow rice, or to be given rice in return for odd jobs such as helping with transplanting, or to be given as a straight gift, especially among relatives.[103] Mutual cooperation also figured in social activities such as building houses, making merit, entering monkhood, and arranging marriages, funerals, and festivals. There were also resources which the village community held together in common and joined together to look after, such as ponds, temples, and forests.[104] Lastly, joining together as a village meant cooperating to prevent any threats to the village. In an old Isan literary work in poetic form, a grandfather teaches his grandchildren: "a lot of people living together is better than a few. It makes little people feel warm. Living together has thousands of merits."[105] When asked to define the word "village" in an interview, one villager replied that a village was "many people settled together, building together, looking after things together, helping to share pain and suffering and to share food to eat".[106] In the past, the word *ban* (house) also meant "village", because there were no houses standing alone without other houses grouped around. Each family which lived in a house was called a *ruan* or *khrua ruan* (household).[107]

The blood relations between members of the village community were another factor contributing to the strength of the internal bonds within the village. This factor was passed down from the tribal community based on kinship relations. The trace of society based on blood relations remained in Upper Siam in the practice of passing down names and family names in the female line, on grounds that the females were the people who reproduced the labour by producing children to replace old labour. At marriage, the male side had to come and pay respects to the spirits of the ancestors of the female side. Inheritance passed through the female line but crossed to the male line if there were no relations on the female side.[108] This principle of social organisation gradually faded away but the remaining traces indicate the kin-based nature of ancient Thai society. Even at present in relatively isolated villages with no contact with other villages and the outside world, members of the community are still mostly related.[109] In addition, another important trace of the society based on blood relations is still found in the practice of quasi-kin relations. Villagers often like to refer to each other with words denoting kin ties. The point is to make the village appear as a unity formed by people who are related together.[110] The leader of the village is called the *pho ban*, father of the village, again recalling the idea that the village developed from a family.[111] Some old proverbs reflect the importance of kin relations and the need to be cautious towards strangers, for instance: *mai ruchak hua non plai tin* "we don't know where he puts his head or his feet when he sleeps",[112] and *roi pho phan mae* "a hundred fathers, a thousand mothers".[113]

The process of class division inside the village emerged slowly in the sakdina period. In part, this was due to the lack of technological development, and in part due to the mutual cooperation, kin ties, and quasi-kin ties. During the sakdina period, there were already landless people but they were still not so numerous. They might be people who had recently moved to the village, or they might be descended from ancestors who were poor. However, they could ask for food from relatives, and sometimes worked for hire, such as in paddy farming, sawing wood, building houses, boiling salt, boiling sugar, and making rope. Otherwise they might gather forest produce. The point is that the landless in the village could find work within the village and did not have to break away.[114] Besides, there was still uncultivated land available in the forest which the landless could claim. If an old village became over-populated, some families might move to find new land to clear, converting forest into paddy field.

In village society under the sakdina system there were also slaves. Bishop Pallegoix estimated that slaves were about one quarter of the Thai population in the Fourth Reign.[115] Slaves were created as a result of debts contracted because of successive crop failures, or because of gambling. A villagers' saying was *pen ni pen kha*, "being indebted is being enslaved".[116] Borrowers often had no way to repay interest. They would first sell their cattle and buffaloes, then their wives and children, then themselves. They could not sell their land because it belonged to the king.[117] Such debt slavery was found mostly around the towns especially in the central region. Slaves in other regions were often war captives, for example Burmese or minority peoples like the Kha, Khamu, Thin, and hill peoples who the Thai captured as whole families to become slaves.[118] Slaves were used in various ways both outside and inside the house—paddy farming, gardening, paddling boats, threshing, clearing grass, feeding buffaloes, beating metal, collecting vegetables, fishing, picking tamarind, picking coconuts, cooking, housework—to the extent there was an old saying, *chai kan yang ka tat*, "being used like a slave".[119] But Thai sakdina society cannot be considered a slave society. There were no large plantations or mines using slave labour. Holders of important government posts might have no more than ten slave families and rich farmers might have just one or two families.[120] Furthermore, slaves were treated like members of the family. Sometimes relatives became slaves in their own family. The master provided food and clothing, and allowed the slaves to build a hut at the end of the plot. Slaves felt bound to their masters and accepted their situation. Even though they had no freedom, had no factors of production, had to work hard, and had no free time, they still did not split away from the master's family and away from the community.[121] Hence slaveholding in Thai sakdina society did not affect the internal bonds within the village community.

One very important feature of sakdina society was that the village community took care to maintain and strengthen the internal bonds. The system of private property right was not yet solidly established, and the trend to division of labour had not progressed far. The state had come into existence, and had its centre outside the village. The important relationship then was between the village and the state, between the class of farmers and the class of government officials, not between individual landowners and individual farmers. There was still no strong urban bourgeois class—the leaders of change in the European feudal system. Under this direct relationship between the sakdina state and the village, the state claimed to protect the village from attack by other states, to provide public services such as communications (digging canals), and to promote Buddhism. But in reality, the state exploited the village. The state was alienated from the village rather than being at one with the village. The corvée system was the most important direct relationship between state and village, and here conflict between the benefit to the state and the benefit to the village was clearly visible. The state needed corvée labour to build forts, camps, palaces, temples, roads, granaries, and crematoria; to dig canals and construct other public works; to make warships and weapons; to work as soldiers and boatmen; to transport nobles and their baggage; and much more besides.[122] But villagers feared corvée more than anything else. They had to leave their village and family behind; they had to take along their own food; often they were starved and had to live on shoots; they were scolded and whipped. If they had to transport nobles and baggage through the forest and mountains, they seriously risked death from fever. Hundreds died in this way on corvée duty.[123] John Crawfurd, ambassador of the East India Company, who visited Siam during the Second Reign, wrote that corvée was a cruelly oppressive system.[124] During the Fourth and Fifth Reigns of the Rattanakosin period, villagers had to render corvée for three months of the year, plus special corvée duties on top for urgent construction work, or for transporting nobles and their baggage through the forest and mountain.[125] Corvée was found in every region of Siam. In the upcountry provinces, villagers often had to perform the corvée labour in the provincial towns.[126] Those who lived in remote areas might send produce taxes instead, or pay a capitation tax if they had the cash. But in a subsistence economy, those who had the capacity to pay government taxes in cash were limited in number.

Villagers feared the corvée. Sometimes whole villages resisted by running away into the forest. The state periodically sent out a force to tattoo numbers on the wrists of those liable for corvée. This force would surround the village and block escape routes, using tactics similar to hunting animals.[127] An old man of 101 years in Ban Nala, tambon Mai Fat, amphoe Sikao, Trang, recounted that eighty-five years ago the Nala villagers were taken to work on corvée. They were given no food and were whipped. The women left behind at home also faced difficulty because they had nothing to eat. In some cases, wives and children starved to death. The old man said: "We were trying to make a living but were not free to do so. The lord took us away to work and work only. It was too oppressive, it was torture." All the villagers along with villagers from Khlong Yao, Lanta island, over a hundred households, fled the corvée by boat to Langkawi island in Malaya. They stayed there twenty years and then returned.[128] There were many other ways to flee the corvée, for instance avoiding work by feigning not to understand, or working slowly; entering the monkhood; or hiding at home.[129] If resistance was strong, it could break out into rebellion. Revolts arose from time to time, especially in Isan at the start of this century when the power of the central state penetrated into the countryside.[130] In sum, although villages were able to maintain their internal structure and bonds, they had to deliver corvée labour and taxes to the state in a systematic way and in gradually increasing amounts. The state grew stronger, and the class of government nobles was securely in the position to dominate Thai sakdina society.

Within the village community with its strong internal bonds, the emergence of a local bourgeois class was blocked. The traders and local artisans, who were the potential buds of a Thai bourgeois class, were not able to develop beyond being farmers, and were not able to develop villages with specific production, such as weaving for sale. The local traders in the north were cattle traders. They transported *miang* (fermented tea), tobacco, and lac out of the village to sell, and brought into the village goods from outside such as dried fish, matches, kerosene, cloth, garments, and salt. The trading routes included: Samoeng to Hot and Wang Lung; Wiangpapao to Chiang Mai; Phrae to Chiang Mai; and Phrao to Chiang Mai. The northern cattle traders concentrated their activity in the north and did not cross into the central region.[131] The local traders in the northeast were the *nai hoi*. They brought cattle and buffalo from the northeast to sell in the central region, or brought trade goods from the forest to sell in the hub towns in Isan itself, the most important being Korat. The products brought for sale included hides, horns, and lac. Along the banks of the Mekong, boat traders sold *pla ra* (fermented fish).[132] In the south there was sale of cut rattan, dried betelnut, and dried coconut. In other words, there was some collection of goods for sale besides the collection for tax payment.[133] These goods gave the villages some small income in cash to buy necessities such as cloth and garments, salt, and rice in times of scarcity. When the cattle traders and *nai hoi* made some surplus from trading, they bought land, made merit, and used all the money up. Besides, they did not trade as their main occupation, but only once a year during the dry season.[134] Chusit Chuchat has made a very broad study of the cattle traders, based on interviews with eighty people who were cattle traders in the past. He concludes that 95 percent of cattle traders wanted to live in the village and only 5 percent wanted to settle in the town. They said "the town is lonely". Besides, since they traded only on a seasonal basis, they did not have the funds needed to shift their location.[135] As for Isan, an ethnic Chinese trader who had established roots in Isan for a long time gave the impression that only 10 percent of the *nai hoi* moved to settle in town.[136] The fact that the cattle traders and *nai hoi* still grew paddy as their main occupation and did not move to settle outside the village prevented the development of a class. They could not make the leap of development into a class separate from the rice farmers. In the central region, the picture was no different. Here the traders were mostly females. They traded by boat along the water courses. The goods they sold were mostly fruit from orchards in places such as Bang Plama, Suphanburi. There were also local traders, both male and female, who went by boat to buy bananas and areo-resin (*namman yang*—used for wicks) at Nakhon Sawan, and who boated down to Bang Len in Nakhon Pathom to buy sugar and coconut for sale to villagers. This was a supplementary occupation, carried out in groups of two or three people working over several days. But only very few people became rich from this sort of trading.[137] Hence in the pre-Bowring period, when the Chinese had not yet penetrated into the village to trade but had only settled in the important hub towns of the central region, full-time local traders who bought and sold as their sole profession had not emerged within the sakdina mode of production.

Siam's lack of a professional trading class can also be seen in long-distance trade, which reached the village only very occasionally. The traders were Kula (Thai Yai) and Tongsu (Iko). They travelled on foot in groups of five to ten persons, bringing foreign goods such as knives, lacquerware, cloth, and dyestuffs from Burma to sell in the central region and Isan. These peoples were Siam's long-distance traders who penetrated into the village long before the Chinese brought imported goods to sell in the village.[138]

Local artisans—such as metalworkers, carpenters, potters, and the brass workers who made the special container for *khanom chin*—did not practice their craft as a sole occupation. They had to grow paddy also, and only worked as artisans when they had time free from the paddy fields. There was no division of labour between artisan work and farming.[139] Even for the production of necessities such as salt, there was no need for the emergence of specialised producers or traders in Isan. It was common for half a village to migrate to the salt fields. For instance, in the dry season the villagers of Kusuman, Sakon Nakhon, went to the salt fields at Na Phliang, one day's walk away. They stayed for one to two months, and then returned. They took their rice along with them, and made temporary shelters like those put up for merit-making festivals.[140] The villagers were self-sufficient in salt as salt lakes were treated as commons and were found all over Isan—such as at Ban Naphin, Ubon Ratchathani; Ban Bo Pho, Loei; and amphoe Sisongkhram, Nakhon Phanom. In the north, there were salt lakes at amphoe Bua, Nan, but they were controlled by the ruler of Nan.[141]

The old pattern of production depended on mutual cooperation between villages, and also on exchange of labour between villages.[142] Moreover, in some places villages also cooperated in exchange of products as well because certain villages were not able to achieve a high degree of self-sufficiency. For example some of the fishing villages on the western coast of the southern region could not plant their own rice. They had to catch fish to exchange for rice with the paddy-farming villages further inland.[143] Villages on the banks of the Mekong river around amphoe Sisongkhram could not plant rice because of the heavy flooding. They made fermented fish to exchange for rice with the paddy-farming villages deeper inland.[144] Some villages in the hills of the north, the western central region, and Isan had to bring vegetables and forest produce to exchange for rice with villages on the plains.[145] In the south, villages which produced fruit at the edge of the hills, had to travel by boats known as *rua neua* or *rua kalang* to exchange fruit for rice and seafood with plains villages.[146] Cooperation between villages could also take other forms. After the rice season was over, people from Pak Phanang, Nakhon Sithammarat, took their cattle and buffalo to Lan Saka and left them there to escape the flooding. The people of Lan Saka were rewarded with rice from Pak Phanang.[147] In this cooperation between villages, one family often built up friendly bonds with a family in the other village. In the north and Isan this was known as *phuk sieo* (tying friendship)[148] and in the south as *mat kloe* (binding pals).[149] These links between families often lasted for several generations, with the exchange of goods continuing with compassion and friendship. Often these relationships crossed ethnic groups as well, such as between the Kha and Phu Tai. The Kha brought rattan, bamboo shoots, and *phak wan* [*Sauropus albicans*, a forest vegetable] to exchange for rice, fish, fermented fish, and salt with the Phu Tai at the edge of the forest.[150]

Besides exchange of goods, in both north and south there was small-scale trade between one village and another, or between village and town, carried out at periodic markets (*talat nat*). At these periodic markets, products from the village included vegetables, beef, pork, chicken, fish, fruit, and products from the outside included cloth, yarn, crockery, and matches. In the past these markets did not happen every day but less regularly, such as one day per week, circulating round various locations. For instance in the north in 1888, James McCarthy reported that only in Chiang Mai was there a market every day.[151] At amphoe Yantakhao, Trang, the frequency used to be two days a week and only thirty years ago became every day.[152] Periodic markets are also found in Sipsongpanna and the Shan States to this day.[153] In Isan, there were no such periodic markets. This system of periodic markets, besides demonstrating the mutual cooperation between villages, also indicates that the old Thai rural economy was a subsistence economy with basic trading carried out only on an occasional basis. Moreover, Isan was the most closed of the regions since it had no rural level markets of any type, only barter of goods for goods. Both barter and occasional markets indicate that subsistence production does not have the strict meaning that there is no exchange or trade. The important point is whether production is mainly for subsistence. There may still be some small-scale trade to achieve sufficiency in necessities, and there may be collection of extra goods for government tax from which there may also be a small surplus for sale, depending on the specific nature of the village in each location.

The Thai sakdina economy was thus an economy with no trading towns, no trading class, no artisan towns, and no artisans. Even Bangkok, which was Siam's centre for overseas trade, had risen primarily as a centre of administration. Several towns of sakdina-period Siam were by nature administrative and religio-cultural centres—bases for the extension of the state's power both in administration and belief. They were the sites of army units, bureaucratic offices, and royal temples to house relics of the Buddha. In the Ayutthaya period, their purpose was to administer tax, to maintain the peace and order of the countryside, and to extend domination over the beliefs of the villages. From the late Ayutthaya period onwards, the first-rank towns of Siam were Phitsanulok and Nakhon Sithammarat. Overseas trade with China, Malaya, and Singapore was on the increase. More Chinese came to settle in Siam. As they were not obliged to render corvée, the Chinese could conveniently practise trading. In particular they took up duties as boatmen, tax collectors, traders in monopoly goods such as opium and liquor on behalf of the government, and planters of commercial crops for export such as sugarcane and pepper. Bangkok and surrounding towns such as Nakhon Chaisi, Ayutthaya, Prachinburi, Chanthaburi, and Ratchaburi developed production and trade for export, especially sugar in Nakhon Chaisi and pepper in Chanthaburi. Even before the Bowring treaty opened up the country, Bangkok and some surrounding towns began to acquire the character of trading towns and centres of commercial crop production. Also in the south, towns such as

Chumphon, Nakhon Sithammarat, Phuket, and Saiburi prospered in the same way from production and trade in tin and birds' nests.[154] From his study of this subject, Nithi Eosiwong concludes that Bangkok and these surrounding towns flourished in the early Rattanakosin period, and that individualism surfaced in the literature of the period to some extent.[155] While Nithi may be correct in identifying change of this nature, the growth in trading towns during the sakdina period was limited to the towns indicated. Even at the end of the Fifth Reign, fifty years after the country had been opened for trade, the Chinese community was still concentrated in Bangkok, Nakhon Chaisi, Ayutthaya, Prachinburi, and Ratchaburi—that is in the central region around Bangkok. The Chinese in these towns were 81.2 percent of the Chinese in the whole of Siam. Including the towns mentioned in the south raises the figure to 94.3 percent of the Chinese in the whole of Siam.[156] The Chinese communities in the upper central region, north, and Isan were still very small. Moreover, the Chinese in the centre and south had not yet created strong relations with the countryside. They were associated with overseas trade as boatmen, tax-collectors, traders in forest produce, agents of the finance ministry; and producers of commercial export crops (sugarcane and pepper) in limited areas. Trade relations between town and countryside were not yet regular. The nature of town formation in Isan indicates that various towns founded in the period of the First to Fifth Reigns were founded totally for administrative reasons. They had been villages with only forty to fifty houses and were called towns because of the state's definition, not because of their trade or artisans.[157] They were founded as towns because the Bangkok state was spreading its power to control the Isan countryside in a more systematic manner following the defeat of Vientiane in 1828. Examples include Ubon Ratchathani, Khemmarat, Amnat Charoen, Mukdahan, Nakhon Phanom, Kalasin, Khon Kaen, Roi-et, Mahasarakham, Surin and Sisaket.[158]

The ideological belief system of the villagers buttressed the strong internal bonds, self-rule, subsistence economy, and identity of the village community. The foundation of villagers' beliefs was belief in the ancestors. They held that after a person died, the spirit remained to protect, look after, and help the descendants. These spirits were called the house or household spirits. They could be counted back up the descent line as far as memory allowed, "*lai sap lai son*", in many rings and layers.[159] In the north they were called *phi puya* (grandfather and grandmother spirits), and in the south *phi tayai* (same meaning).[160] Minority peoples like the Kha also believed in ancestor spirits, calling them *phi pho phi mae* (spirit of father and mother).[161] Thai villagers kept an ancestor spirit house on a prayer shelf in the bedroom of every family. At the level of the village, there were spirits of the village community. In the north, they were called *phi sua ban* and had a spirit house at the edge of the forest where a big tree still stood close to the village. The spot was called *pa sua ban*.[162] In Isan the village spirits were called *phi puta* and in the same fashion had a spirit house in the forest edge called *dong puta*.[163] Villagers in the Shan States believed that the spirits of the village community resided in the centre post of the house (the house pillar) and they paid respects to the ancestors of the village at this place.[164] Ceremonies were held to give food to the spirits of the village, to drive away other bad spirits, and to maintain the fortune of the village by driving away things which are bad luck. In Lanna Thai and Sipsongpanna villages, they surrounded the village with *ta laeo*, bamboo woven into an octagon with seven eyes in a row, following the legend that these stand for the eyes of the eagles (*nok laeo*) which were the guardians of the locality in the past. For the three to seven days which the ceremony lasted, nobody could enter or leave the village. This ceremony shows vestiges of the self-rule, identity, and freedom which probably existed in full in the era of the primordial community. In Thai villages of Sipsongpanna, the village territory is still defined by two gates called *khoen ban* which villagers build at the head of the village and in some places attach a piece of wood carved into the shape of a two-edged sword to ward off threats to the village.[165] Localities covering several villages often had a hero spirit—perhaps a fighter, someone important in the locality, or a local lord. Examples in Isan include the Mahesak spirit at Kusuman, Sakon Nakhon;[166] in the north, *chao luang kham* (*daeng*) (lord of gold), *khun luang mae langka*, *chao pho kho mu lek* (spirit lord of the iron wrist);[167] in the south, *phaya saifafat* (lord lightning rod), *phaya luifai* (lord firewalker), and the group of *khru mo* (*mo* in ancient Thai meant teacher), teachers of the Nora dance and music, including *ta luang khong* (grandfather Luang Khong), *ta luang nai* (grandfather Luang Nai), *ta si chum* (grandfather Si Chum);[168] in the central region, *chao pho khun krai* in Suphanburi province.[169] These hero or lord spirits hark back to the period of change from a society of free villages to one of small local principalities with heroes, warriors, and local lords. Villagers have contracted the spirits of these heroes, warriors, and local lords as their own spirits, as spirits of the villagers. Above the spirits of local lords, at the level of state and king, there was no spirit such as the spirit of the Thai nation state to provide help, protection, and assistance. There were only spirits of Thai ethnic groups, not of the state. For instance, *phi thaen* or *phi fa* gave birth to the Thai peoples. *Phi thaen* was called on to help make the rain fall, to enter a human body and dance, to help villagers recover from sickness, be strong and healthy, and to chase away forest spirits.[170] In addition, there were spirits or angels who resided in natural things such as trees, ricefields (*phi ta haek*), rocks, mountains (*phrakhapung phi, to laem, thuat hua hi, thuat hin ru yang, ta luang*, etc.), and rice stalks (*mae phosop*).[171] Villagers believed that these nature spirits—such as *phi pop, phi krasua, phi ka, phi pa* (forest spirit)—could sometimes create harm for the villagers such as making them sick. Also the spirits of the household or ancestors could create unforeseen difficulty if their villager descendants broke ancient customs. This was known as *phit phi*, wronging the spirits. In the world-view of the villagers, sickness, epidemics, natural dangers, and crop failure were explained as the work of spirits who were offended by the behaviour of some families or of the whole village.[172] The belief in ancestral spirits demonstrates how the old village belief in the bloodline and kin group tied together the living, and tied the living together with the ancestors. Belief in ancestral spirits showed the importance of the kin system in the thinking of Thai villagers. Villages retained the vestiges of the system of extended kin or clans. Inhabitants of the one village shared the same ancestral spirits, who were the real elders of the village, who were born within the village itself, and who warded off strange things from outside.

The villagers' creation of spirits indicates the importance which villagers attached to maintaining the system of kin and family and the village community. They believed that members of the village community had strong bonds with one another, shared the same family ancestors, and had to follow closely the ancient customs and advice of the ancestors, or else they would anger the spirits so much that they would provide no protection against dangers from outside the village, and might inflict punishment. The belief in and fear of spirits that resided in nature was one aspect of a society in which knowledge of science and technology was low, and in which natural events were attributed to spirits. This belief made the villagers peaceful and not determined to conquer nature. A foreign cleric wrote about Lanna villagers at the start of this century that if their house roof was blown off in a storm, they did not think this showed they had not built the house well, but believed that the spirits had made it happen that way. If they fell sick, they did not think they had an infection, but again attributed the cause to a spirit.[173] Praying to spirits that resided in nature was praying to nature—surrendering to nature because of having no tools with which to conquer nature. The old belief system of the village was consistent with and supportive of a community with strong internal bonds and a production base which was natural, had low technology, and was oriented to subsistence.

But in the sakdina system, the state had already come into existence. The emergence of the state affected the village in the area of belief and ideology, as well as in the matter of corvée and tax. As in the case of economy and administration, so in the area of belief, the state chose to dominate the village in one aspect—that aspect which bore on relations between the village and the state, between the farmer class and the sakdina class. The state left other aspects of belief concerned with the everyday life of villagers to continue as before or with just some limited adjustment. Buddhist beliefs were blended in with beliefs in village spirits, allowing spirit belief to remain central.[174] With respect to the relations between village and state, farmer class and sakdina class, Buddhism was used to explain and legitimate the rise of the sakdina class as rulers. The system of belief in ancestors and the blood line of kin provided no explanation for the difference between the two classes. It could not explain why the lords and rulers should use corvée labour and should receive *suai* tax from the villagers. In the system of belief in ancestors, people in society were related to one another and were equal to one another. There were no classes of rulers and ruled, no class which could take tax from another class. To explain the legitimacy of the state to rule and extract resources from the village, the state used the principle of merit and karma in Buddhism: villagers faced difficulty, poverty, hunger, and misery because they had sinned in a previous life, while the lords and nobles had accumulated merit in the past. As monks said in sermon, *bun ko tong um pai*, merit must carry him forward.[175] A village saying ran: "they have the good fortune to be lords and masters, we are ordinary people with a lesser fortune".[176] This indicates that villagers tended to accept the explanation of the legitimacy of the emergence of a sakdina class which was distinct from themselves. At the same time, this acceptance made villagers afraid of people who had higher merit and power (*barami*).[177] One clear example of the domination of village ideology from outside the village was the statement of a Kha man aged 103 years at Ban Dong Luang, amphoe Dong Luang, Nakhon Phanom. When asked who the Kha were, he replied: "Kha are the servants of Buddha. They offer no challenge. I'm simple, I'm stupid."[178] On the relation between the state's exploitation of the village and the village mentality, Kanoksak Kaewthep summed up excellently that: "It's not that farmers cannot see the exploitation or do not feel exploited. Just the opposite. In reality farmers feel exploited. But the farmers explain to themselves that the reason behind this exploitation is that they lack 'merit.'"[179]

The state used Buddhism to make villagers accept the class of state nobles. But apart from this, the state had no interest whether Buddhism should become a real element of the life of the villagers or not. And the villagers' old belief in spirits opposed the intervention of religion into the daily life within the village.

Hence under the sakdina system, spirit belief remained central to the village, and Buddhism had to adjust to fit with local beliefs. Especially in Upper Siam, in the north and Isan, spirit belief was stronger than Buddhism in everyday life. When there was hardship such as sickness or drought, when things went missing, or when people had to travel, villagers would pray to spirits rather than going to see the monks.[180] A foreign cleric summed up in 1901 that "spirit worship is today, as it ever has been, the real religion of the Laos people".[181] Buddhism was given a local character, for instance by blending spirit worship into Buddhist ceremonies, or by transforming local ceremonies into Buddhist ceremonies—such as the frog and fish chants in ceremonies calling for rain in Isan. In some places, the monks paid respect to the local spirits, or believed in the emergence of local holy men (*phumibun*).[182] In some localities, Buddhism has not yet become established. Some minorities still worship only spirits.[183] Local village beliefs which have been preserved in some cases have served as the ideological basis for disputes with the state. When mixed with the desire to maintain the self-rule and subsistence economy of the village, such beliefs occasionally exploded into revolts by ethnic minorities, especially in places where the state intervened more and more heavily into a community which previously lay at the periphery of state power. Such revolts include the Yan Phichian revolt, Bun Kwang revolt, and several Kha revolts (Chiang Kaeo 1791, Sakiet Ngong 1820).[184] But usually the sakdina system was peaceful. The village allowed the state to take corvée labour and produce taxes. The bourgeois class and its liberal ideology were weak and did not spread. Farmers still retained beliefs along the lines of the anarchic socialism of the primordial village, but these beliefs were not manifested clearly and strongly to the point they were a danger to the state. The identity and internal beliefs of the village community were preserved right though the sakdina period. The villagers' opposition to the state mostly took the form of indifference—slacking and playing around on corvée duty, or uprooting the village and fleeing into the forest.

# CHAPTER THREE

# FROM SUBSISTENCE VILLAGE ECONOMY TO COMMERCIAL ECONOMY IN THE CENTRAL REGION, 1855–1932

AFTER the Bowring Treaty of 1855, the monopoly trade run by the Siamese ministry of finance was replaced by free trade. At the same time the demand for rice, Siam's principal product, began to increase rapidly as Western imperial powers needed rice to feed their Southeast Asian colonial territories which concentrated on production of sugar, tin, and jute.[1] Siam's rice production increased sharply in the period 1870–1900. The cultivated area under rice expanded from around 5.8 million *rai* in 1850 to 9.2 million *rai* in 1905–9.[2] Rice exports grew similarly fast. In the period 1870 to 1910, they grew at 5 percent a year, and from 1909–10 to 1938–39 at 1.5 percent a year.[3] The volume of rice exports grew from 2.4 million piculs (picul=60 kg) in 1864 to 8.1 million in 1890.[4] From the end of the nineteenth century onwards, rice became Siam's first-ranked export product.[5] In 1870, exports were only 5 percent of total rice production, but by 1907 they were 40 percent.[6]

These statistics tally with the impressions of contemporary observers who wrote that the period after the Bowring treaty was different from the period before. Prince Dilok Nopparat, a son of King Chulalongkorn, wrote in a thesis in 1907 that: "previously paddy farming was not so widespread as at the present time for the reason that the king used to ban rice exports then". He noted further that "overseas trade... began to have real importance in the nineteenth century, as a result of King Mongkut concluding trade treaties with many countries. These treaties were like opening the door for many agricultural and forest products to flow out of the country to world markets."[7] Almost all countries of Southeast Asia underwent this shift towards an export economy at around the same time towards the end of the nineteenth century because the capitalist countries extended their power and needed local products for trade.

The increase of rice production for export resulted mostly from extension of production in the central region. J. Homan van der Heide estimated that at the start of this century, around 1905–6, 98 percent of Siamese rice exports came from the central region, only 1 percent came from the north, and the same from the northeast.[8] In 1907 he stated that the central region was the market with the highest potential for economic development since this region accounted for 40 percent of the country's total population but 80 percent of total exports (including products other than rice, especially tin and teak), 90 percent of imports, and 80 percent of the state's total tax revenue.[9] James C. Ingram, the economic historian, stated that in 1905–9 the total area of rice cultivation in Siam was 9.2 million *rai*, with 6.8 million in the central region and 2.4 million in other regions combined. In 1925–29 the total area of rice cultivation was 18.1 million *rai*, with 10.9 million in the central region and 7.2 million in other regions combined.[10] When Professor Carle C. Zimmerman made a rural economic survey of Siam in 1930, he stated: "Since Siam was opened to foreign trade, there has been a marked change in the economic practices of the country districts in the central plains."[11] He gave figures that farm plots in the central region were in the range of 30–200 *rai*, which was very different from Isan and the south where plots were only 1–20 *rai*.[12] Zimmerman concluded that Siam in 1930 had only one area of commercial economy and that was the central region, while Isan and the south still had subsistence economies. The north was semi-subsistence, semi-commercial.[13] Based on figures from village sample surveys, Zimmerman estimated that farmers' cash income per family was 279 baht per year in the central region, 176 baht in the north, 126 baht in the south, and 83 baht in Isan. In the north, south, and Isan, trading was limited to areas close to the main towns and main communication routes.[14]

Interviews with village elders give a picture of the same nature as the surveys of Professor Zimmerman, the writings of van der Heide, and the estimates of Professor Ingram. These interviews show that farmers in the central region had grown paddy for sale for a long time—from the time of the interviewees' grandfathers or before. This means the central region grew paddy for sale from the later nineteenth century, while other regions only began commercial production later during the twentieth century.

Statistics from the period 1907/8–1909/10 show that 50 percent of the rice production of the whole country was exported.[15] As this figure is calculated from the whole country, the percentage for the central region alone would be higher. Professor Zimmerman estimated that in 1930–31, three-fifths of the rice grown in the central region was sold.[16] In the latter half of the century after the Bowring treaty, the village economy of the central region had gone through a fundamental change. Rice production mainly for subsistence had become production for sale as well. The economy had changed from subsistence to commercial as a result of the demand from the capitalist economy outside the country. The village economy of the central region had been tied to the metropolitan capitalist system which extended its boundaries into Asia through the rice trade.

The expansion of commercial rice production in the central region took the form of extending the cultivated area, not increasing productivity. In the past paddy was grown in the areas of Suphanburi, Singburi, Inburi, Phromburi, and northwards from Ayutthaya.[17] During the Fourth Reign, Bishop Pallegoix wrote that "on ne cultive pas la moitié de la plaine" (less than half of the plains is cultivated).[18] However, towards the end of the nineteenth century, farmers in the central region migrated to cultivate in the area of the lower Chaophraya delta, both left and right banks. On the left bank, the important area was Rangsit which before was a swamp.[19] In the 1890s, the Siam Land, Canals, and Irrigation Company contracted to dig canals to open up this tract for paddy farming. Farmers moved from around Samut Sakhon and Samut Songkhram where some of the land was saline because of inroads of sea water. Also slaves who had been liberated by the nobles moved in to settle and farm.[20] In the right bank tract of the Chaophraya, to the west of Ayutthaya and east of Suphanburi, the area was very low-lying with flood water for many months of the year. Earlier, people from the northern part of the central region had come to plant paddy but returned home at the end of each season. At the end of the nineteenth century, they began to settle.[21] Canals were dug out from the river, including Mahasawat (1861), Prem Prachakon (1870), Prawet Burirom (1880), Damnoen Saduak (1898), and the Rangsit canal system (1890s). These canals helped to drain away flood water and also acted as transport routes to move rice out to market. People moved in to settle permanently. Kitti Tanthai estimated that new canals dug in the lower central region in the period 1870–1904 opened up at least 1.3 million *rai* for paddy growing.[22] Sunthari Asawai estimated that the figure may be 2 million *rai* since she included the 700,000 *rai* of land under the second stage of the Rangsit project.[23] This movement to settle and grow paddy in the delta tract where previously cultivation had been shifting, took place also in Burma and Vietnam, with the Thai case happening slightly later than the neighbouring countries.[24] In addition, paddy cultivation also expanded into upland areas which had been forested, such as the west of Ratchaburi province, amphoe Lat Yao in Nakhon Sawan, amphoe Khok Samrong in Lopburi, and amphoe Uthong in Suphanburi.[25]

The extension of the cultivated area under paddy in the later nineteenth century was made possible also by the liberation of the Thai population from the corvée system, and the introduction instead of a capitation tax (as a full system from the Capitation Tax Act of 1910) and army conscription (1905). In addition, the abolition of slavery (beginning from 1874) over the same period made possible the movement of people to settle and cultivate in the newly opened tracts. The abolition of the corvée system meant that the village no longer had to deliver up labour services. Rice taxes in kind had already been replaced by land tax from 1824 in the Third Reign. Hence under the new system villagers paid taxes to the state in the form of cash. Individual freedom increased. But at the same time, tax payment in cash forced the villagers to enter more into the capitalist system.

At the same time, the old existing property system under which the state was the sole landowner began to weaken. The land which the king had conferred on nobles was not recalled. In 1860 during the Fourth Reign, an act laid down that the state had to pay cash compensation to the occupant of land which the state assumed.[26] At the village level, the migration and extension of cultivation in the central region, especially in the lowlands of the Chaophraya delta, led to the foundation of new villages often composed of peoples from various localities. These villages were often shaped in long strips along the banks of a river or canal. The form of landholding tied to membership of the village community weakened to some extent, while the system of private property rights in land strengthened. Those who occupied new lands in the central region, whether they were nobles or villagers, began to claim that they were the individual owners of each piece of land. The livelihood of the rural villagers still depended on the village community as before. Yet in the second half of the nineteenth century, throughout the central region there emerged a system of small free peasants who were owners of their modest plots. This was possible because there was enough land available to claim outside the system of large-scale landholdings which nobles received from the king along the banks of the rivers and newly dug canals, and which the nobles rented to their liberated slaves and *phrai* to make a livelihood.

However, in interviews one important point emerged about rice production in the central region which does not appear in Ingram, Zimmerman, or van der Heide. Commercial rice production in the central region began in the first place as a supplementary activity to production for own consumption. When asked about the extent of their rice production for sale at the end of the nineteenth and start of the twentieth century, elders mostly replied that they kept back enough rice for food and for seed before selling the surplus. Alternatively they waited until they could see the rice ripened in the following season, or until the new crop was harvested, before they sold the old crop. This was known as *hen nong chung cha khai*, "seeing the younger one before selling".[27] Because villagers in this period grew for own consumption as their first priority and sold only the real surplus which fluctuated from year to year, the conversion towards mono-production at the village level, even in the central region, was not rapid. Although the volume of rice exports increased rapidly in this period, farmers treated the sale of rice as a supplementary activity and continued to weave cloth for their own use. Initially farmers were probably not sure whether they would produce enough rice for sale and not sure whether they would have money to buy cloth and other necessities like salt, onions, garlic, betelnut, and yarn. The income from rice sale was not yet certain. Hence farmers still kept up weaving through the period when the sale of rice increased.

Weaving for own use in the central region declined slowly. Spinning of yarn disappeared first and yarn for weaving was purchased. Yet spinning only ceased after the Second World War in some localities such as amphoe Ban Mi, Lopburi, and Uttaradit, especially amphoes Nam Pak and Fak Tha.[28] Weaving in the central region survived through the end of the nineteenth century and start of the twentieth but declined gradually and had almost disappeared by the start of the Second World War in 1941. But the war created a shortage of imported cloth which made weaving for own use continue through the war and disappear at the war's end.[29] The popularity of weaving for own use was most obvious in village communities of a special ethnic background such as Lao Phuan, Lao Song, and Mon which preserved weaving for own use longer. For instance, in the Lao Song community of amphoe Chombung, Ratchaburi, weaving for own use ceased only twenty years ago. In Lao Song communities in Phetchaburi it still survives in the present day.[30] In many central region villages it is still possible to see old weaving equipment such as looms and spinning wheels kept by the villagers. These show that weaving for own use in the central region is not something ancient and remote as was once understood and as was portrayed in Ingram, van der Heide, and the work I wrote with Suthy Prasartset, which argued that the local weaving industry in the central region disintegrated immediately after the opening of the country in the mid-nineteenth century. Based on interviews and surveys at the village level, the correct picture is that the village craft of weaving disappeared slowly from the central region, or as the villagers put it, *mot pai duai priyai* (died slowly of natural causes),[31] and that the true end came a hundred years after the opening of the country. However, while villagers were still weaving for own use, once they were able to sell rice they also bought garments. They used cash to buy clothes to wear at festivals and kept the cloth woven by themselves to wear at home. The fact that villagers still wove for own use even after they began producing rice for sale in large quantities, shows that they were not confident about the trading they were involved in. The implication is that the villagers were dragged into the market system, into the capitalist system, and were half-hearted about it.

The use of old production methods and technology in rice production— human labour and animals—and the expansion of production volume by extension of the cultivated area, indicate the antiquated state of the village community's productive power. The pattern was the same as when villagers had sought an easy livelihood from nature by fishing, hunting, and gathering fruit and vegetables. For labour, they used family members, supplemented by *long khaek* exchange labour for peak demands such as transplanting and harvesting. Wage labour began in the central region at the very end of the nineteenth century. Agricultural wage labourers came from Isan on a temporary basis. Chinese labour worked on clearing forest, digging out stumps, and digging ponds. Poor landless people in the villages worked as wage labour for digging and farming.[32] But exchange labour was still in widespread use up to the end of the Second World War, and was only gradually replaced by wage labour. In some places such as Phichit, exchange labour disappeared only twenty or more years ago.[33] The old style of production persisted in the practice of pounding rice for eating which used heavy manual labour several times a day. In Ayutthaya pounding rice disappeared only thirty to forty years ago, and the mortars still exist.[34] At tambon Don Khlang, amphoe Damnoen Saduak, Ratchaburi, pounding of rice disappeared only twenty years ago.[35] The long survival of weaving for own use and these other practices shows that the village community was dragged rapidly into the commercial system but failed to adjust to this external impact in time. As a result, villagers preserved the old structure of production as insurance. Many features of the subsistence economy persisted. The subsistence economy resisted changing into a commercial economy, even in the central region where changes extended over a broad area.

Production for sale in the central region gave rise to new classes who moved in to trade and put down roots in the localities. The Chinese merchants became closely involved in the village economy. Previously, the Chinese had come into the localities in certain specific roles: as tax farmers who had monopoly rights from the state over certain forms of trade such as Chinese sweetmeats (*khanom chan ap* made from puffed rice, candied white gourd, sugared peanut), liquor, opium and gambling dens; as collectors of transit taxes on products such as fruit and vegetables;[36] and as boatmen who paddled along the waterways selling groceries such as salt, onions, garlic, betelnut, and yarn. But the Chinese did not settle,[37] except for those who planted commercial crops like sugarcane and pepper, and they were confined to limited areas such as Nakhon Chaisi (sugarcane), Phichit (sugarcane), and Chanthaburi (pepper).[38] But after commercial rice production developed, the Chinese began to settle. They established rafts or shops at the junctions of the waterways and travelled to buy rice. Such settlements appeared along the Chaophraya river system at places like Ayutthaya, Pa Mok, Ang Thong, Singburi, Nakhon Sawan, and Paknampho, and along the Pasak river system at Saraburi and Sao Hai.[39] The Chinese who flooded in during the nineteenth century as coolie labour and tried to change their status to traders, had to settle and trade deep in from the main waterways along the canals and in the big villages. The tax farmers who had arrived earlier traded in Bangkok and the major hub towns, using the money made from tax as capital.[40] The markets along the banks of the Chaophraya prospered. Some places developed into important trading towns, including Paknampho which became the largest rice market outside Bangkok.[41] The Chinese trading community spread out from its old locations in the towns around Bangkok to congregate in various places along the Chaophraya, Pasak, Thachin, and Bang Pakong river systems in the central region. They gradually moved northwards and out along the canals connected to these rivers. The investment capital of this class of ethnic Chinese traders was accumulated in Siam during the later nineteenth and early twentieth century. It was not brought from China. The Chinese truly came to Siam in the style of "one pillow and one mat" and made their starting capital in various ways: saving money from wage labour, getting help in some cases from the side of a Thai wife, getting help from village families who had a decent livelihood, benefiting from the privileges of working for the government as tax farmers, and so on.[42] "They lived off us Thai, or else how did they become rich".[43] Most importantly they were hard-working and frugal, as the Thai villagers say rather angrily: "They never let on whether they are making a lot or a little. They only collect. They know how to save and hoard."[44]

The Chinese traders who settled in the localities, especially in the markets along the rivers and canals, can be divided into two occupational groups. The first sold groceries and imported goods brought from Bangkok. The second purchased rice to sell on to the rice barges. There may have been some merchants who carried on both trades at the same time but they were few in number. For the most part, the two groups were separate. The first group sold salt, fish sauce, onions, shrimp paste, chilli, garlic, betelnut, brown sugar, white sugar, sickles, kerosene, clothing, and food such as noodles, pork, and rice and curry.[45] They acted as middlemen conveying goods into the villages. They connected the foreign stores in Bangkok to a trade network which penetrated to the village. They sold clothing which slowly undermined local craft production. The second group of paddy traders paddled boats or rode bullock carts into the villages to buy up the paddy. They then stored the paddy until the rainy season (September–November) when rice barges came to buy paddy by the boatload (of about twenty *kwian*). During the rainy season, they bought and sold on to the rice barges straightaway.[46] Even in the twentieth century after the arrival of the railway during the Seventh Reign, 86 percent of rice still moved to Bangkok by water and only 14 percent by rail.[47] The assembly points for paddy barges were at Paknampho and Ayutthaya,[48] where the Phichit (Yom and Nan) and

Pasak tributaries join with the Chaophraya river. Paddy was conveyed to the rice mills in Bangkok for milling into rice for consumption in the city and for export. In the later nineteenth century, most of the rice mills were in Bangkok. Until 1919 there were only fifty-six electrified rice mills, with thirty-seven in and around Bangkok, seven in the south, and the rest scattered around.[49] Significantly, Thai villagers did not trade and transport paddy to the barges themselves. Neither did they have any large-scale granaries for storing rice to wait for a good price. The Chinese took up the role of middlemen. Some Thais tried the role of trader and middleman in the rice trade but generally they did not succeed because they worked as both farmer and trader without taking the decision to specialise in one activity.[50] The village women who sold orchard fruit by boat did not enter into the rice trade. Hence the traders who bought paddy were all Chinese. The expansion of commercial rice production created a new class whose role was to connect the village to the capitalist system. The capitalist system penetrated into the village along with the settlement of the Chinese traders. This was different from the colonised countries where capitalism penetrated with the expansion of large-scale foreign plantations.

The further development of the Chinese merchant class in the central region localities in the period from the 1920s, or the end of the Sixth Reign, up to the Second World War took two directions. First, some paddy merchants and industrialists such as brick-makers joined together to build rice mills in the provinces.[51] Second, some of the grocery and imported goods merchants lent money to the farmers and became both merchants and moneylenders. These two groups were separate because none had the capital to carry out both businesses at the same time and because their interests were different. The rice millers were progressive capitalists. Their interest lay in increasing productive capacity through modern technology and seeking a surplus by increasing the efficiency of the factory. The merchant-moneylenders sought a surplus from exploiting the villagers.

From the start of the twentieth century onwards, central region farmers began to lose land, most significantly from the 1920s. At the end of the nineteenth century when rice was sold for cash, some farmers spent all the proceeds on cloth, on more special foods such as salted fish (*pla thu*), salted crab, betelnut, tobacco, chilli, onion, and garlic, on building houses, and on ordinations and marriages for their children. Ordination ceremonies became very grand affairs and marriages only a little less so. The feasting grew to the extent that a cow or buffalo had to be killed for a wedding, and two or three years would not be enough to pay off the debt incurred by one son's ordination. Some people gambled on cock-fighting and hi-lo, drank liquor, or sometimes wasted money on court cases.[52] Even those who did not spend money on such things faced the problem of droughts and crop or animal disease, and had to borrow money for food from the grocery merchants in the market, or from rich farmers who had saved up and had luckily faced no natural disaster. But the interest rates were high, at up to 50 percent for just the three to four months leading up to the harvest—loans taken in the eleventh or twelfth month and paid back in the second month.[53] These rates made it impossible for farmers to pay off their loans. Sometimes moneylenders used dishonest methods, such as changing a 500 baht loan into 5000 baht, or undercounting the true number of cartloads in cases where the farmers repaid in paddy.[54] This was "living on the back of the people". Phraya Suriyanuwat who wrote the first Thai text on economics (1911) stated that the farmers were "really labouring as if for the benefit of another group of people, really pitiful".[55] Chaophraya Wongsanupraphat, minister of agriculture, wrote to the king in 1910 advising that "sometimes farmers have to sell their paddy cheap even though they know the Chinese merchant is squeezing the price. This happens because they need cash to pay land and head taxes and to pay interest on loans as well. If they don't have cash they will be arrested or have their property such as cattle and buffaloes seized, and their land auctioned off."[56] According to the section of the Three Seals law on loans, someone who refused to redeem a debt was "bound and yoked, steeped in water for three days, and exposed to the sun for three days without shade". [57] Prince Dilok Nopparat (thesis 1907) and Professor Zimmerman (*Rural Economic Survey* 1931) who studied the Thai rural economy in the early twentieth century, both stated that the moneylenders' blood-sucking interest rates and the lack of other sources of credit for the farmers, were the biggest problems of rural Siam at the time.[58] Professor Zimmerman gave figures that in 1930, 49 percent of central region farming families were in debt, mostly to moneylenders rather than relatives and neighbours.[59] Debt also led to loss of land because land had to be placed as collateral for the loans. If the crop failed for two to three years in a row, there would be no money to pay the interest, the interest would be added on to the principal, and at this point the farmers "had it".[60] Interest was more costly than rent, because interest had to be paid in the same fixed amount even if there was a drought or flood. But a rent such as a 50:50 crop share declined in proportion if the paddy yield fell. An old saying of central region farmers was "what flower is more fertile than the money flower".[61] If interest was rolled into the principal, before long the farmer had to transfer the collateral land to the moneylender. A 1923 report by the commissioner of monthon Nakhon Chaisi showed that many villagers in Nakhon Pathom had mortgaged their land to moneylenders. In Suphanburi, villagers had mortgaged their title deeds, occupancy documents, and claims papers for not less than half of the total land. In Ang Thong during the worldwide depression of 1930, 30–40 percent of farmers lost their land because of mortgage.[62] The same happened in other parts of the central region. One section of the farmers became landless as a result of debt. The process of land loss because of debt began at the start of this century, less than one hundred years ago, and intensified from the 1920s, that is, about sixty years ago.

A landowning class began to appear in the Thai countryside along with the gradual dismantling of the system under which the state was the sole owner of land. This class consisted of two main groups. The first were moneylenders from outside the village. They were Chinese grocery traders who accumulated land by seizure because the farmers had no way to repay loans. One of the biggest moneylenders was Kim Liang Wungtan (Luang Sitthepakan) who had landholdings from Ratchaburi to Suphanburi.[63] Other examples were families at Taphan Hin, Phichit and amphoe Phak Hai, Ayutthaya, amphoe Ban Mi, Lopburi, and so on.[64] The second group were lords and nobles who acquired land through the power of the state. Some received land by direct royal grant, such as the land along the banks of the Mahasawat, Prem Prachakon, and Damnoen Saduak canals. Others staked claims or were granted land because they raised its utility by such methods as digging canals or building dams to store water for paddy cultivation. They had monopoly rights from the state and were able to use corvée labour because of their official power. Examples include the land along the Rangsit canal and amphoe Kao Lieo, Nakhon Sawan.[65] At the village level, a landowner class appeared in the same way but on a smaller scale. Mostly these were people who saved, did not drink liquor, did not gamble, and were lucky to escape natural disaster. Alternatively they were relatives of the local officials. This group also lent money and accumulated a lot of land, but on a scale of a few hundred *rai*,[66] not like the two groups above whose holdings ran into thousands of *rai*.

What impact did the emergence of this new class—a bourgeoisie of Chinese origin whose trading activity made them into owners of land in the village—have on the village community? It made the village more dependent on the outside world. A significant portion of the village's major product, rice, was now sold to the external market, and the village bought a portion of its cloth from the outside world. Village production was no longer for subsistence, for food, for own use only, but also for sale. The village was not economically totally self-sufficient as before. It could not achieve reproduction by relying only on itself. However, as already noted, the village still protected itself for a long time by making its own cloth even though it bought the yarn from outside. The new class of Chinese entered into relations with the village that were more continuous and deeper than those of the old official class. Yet close analysis shows that the bourgeois class still used a method of extracting the surplus from the village community which was similar to that of the sakdina state. It took a profit from rice trading, from importing goods into the village from the outside world, and from exploitative moneylending. But it did not enter into management of production along capitalist lines. Rather, it left the village to manage production as it had before. Even though moneylenders and nobles came to own land in the village, they rented it back to the old village families who continued to work together as members of the old community as before and pay rent as arranged (however the link between the villagers and the village through land tenure was affected). They did not use the land they had acquired as plantations. The bourgeois class's method of extracting a surplus from the village was along the lines that Karl Marx called "primitive accumulation of capital"; the capitalist class extracted a surplus from a backward mode of production through trickery or power. The tax farmers extracted a surplus by using state power to gain advantage in trade. The moneylenders' exploitative interest rates and land seizure in many cases depended on local power and influence. Extracting a surplus through exchange or through direct seizure is different from creating a surplus by increasing efficiency. In the former, a more advanced mode of production sucks a surplus from an old mode of production without breaking down its internal structure. In the latter, an old mode of production is developed into a capitalist mode of production by changing the technology of production and the class relations within the old mode of production. The capitalist mode of production that appeared in Thai society in the late nineteenth century used the first method in its contact with the village. Hence the impact on structural change within the village was limited, both in technological development and the rise of new classes in the village. Capitalism could not destroy the village community.

The emergence of a class of landless peasants within the village was a long-term change in Thai society which affected the village community more than the rise of the Chinese bourgeois class. Class differentiation inside the village appeared in the form of one group becoming impoverished, having no land or losing it and becoming renters or rural labour, rather than the process of one group of farmers becoming rich and turning into rural capitalists. The impoverishment of central region farmers to the point of land loss happened from the 1920s onwards with gradually increasing intensity as a result of the increase of population from 4.5–5 million in 1855 to 9.2 million in 1919 and 11.5 million in 1929, or a rate of 2.9 percent a year over 1919–29.[67] The supply of land which could be claimed, cleared, and easily converted into paddy field dwindled. A segment of farmers who faced natural disasters such as successive droughts or floods, or who lost money in gambling and had their land seized because they lacked money to pay debts, became tenants and continued to work their old land which now belonged to the moneylender; or became rural wage labour hired for transplanting, harvesting, digging, and at other times making baskets, hats, and water-dippers to sell in the village.[68] Another group of farm wage labourers were the northeasterners. They initially came temporarily but later some put down roots in the central region, especially in the area of Nakhon Nayok and Chachoengsao. They were also landless and came with just a sickle to work on the harvest.[69] In these ways, a class of landless people appeared in the village. From his survey in 1930, Professor Zimmerman stated that 36 percent of all farming families in the central region were landless.[70] The system of independent peasants claiming land ownership, as in the pioneer age in the second half of the nineteenth century, began to disappear from the countryside of the rural central region within only fifty years. Many small independent farmers lost their freedom and became landless. In the Third World, the rise of a landless rural class affects the institution of the village in the long term since ultimately these people have to seek a living outside the village. Currently in Latin America the village is breaking down because the surplus has been completely sucked away and most of the farmers have had to migrate to the city slums. The process of social transformation is not as smooth as in western Europe because those who move to the city find no work because industry has not developed very much. They find it impossible to send resources back home to support and develop the village. The village deteriorates yet there are no factories to compensate. This parasitic form of capitalist development makes the village decline, breaks down the small community, breaks down the subsistence economy, and at the same time fails to establish a new mode of production. This process lies behind the painful situation which underdeveloped countries experience in the present day.

The emergence of a bourgeois class may modify this negative process if the bourgeois class comes to rely on the peasantry to press for a democratic revolution, carry out land reform, overhaul the old bureaucratic system, and industrialise. In that case, a progressive bourgeoisie may overthrow the parasitic capitalism that develops from exploitation of the countryside, develop industrial capitalism, and allow the countryside to remain in its old state. The result is a balance between the village and the factory, advance in agricultural technology, and farmers' participation in their own development. The Thai capitalist class has not played this role. It developed by taking advantage of the villagers rather than relying on them. The political change of 1932 was not a proper democratic revolution. The peasantry did not take part, and benefited very little. It is difficult for the farmers to free themselves from the sakdina state and from parasitic capitalism with only the power of their own class. The prospect for change in the internal production structure of the village and in the place of the village in the political economy and culture, must be considered in the context of alliances with other social classes. The reason why the Thai countryside changed slowly, fell into decline, was exploited continuously throughout the history of Thai capitalist development, and was neglected rather than supported and protected by the state, lies in the conservatism of the Thai bourgeois class.

Besides the lack of leadership by the bourgeois class, a further reason why the countryside remained peaceful despite the exploitation of the village and the rise of a landless class, lies in the culture and power of the sakdina state. Among the farmers themselves, "the poor accepted the rich", that is accepted their headship.[71] In addition, villagers believed strongly in morality and avoided conflict.[72] In dealings with officials, landowners, and moneylenders, farmers showed both gratitude[73] and fear,[74] even though they might be angry and bitter at being exploited. As soon as the farmers had some paddy, the landowners and moneylenders went right to their house to scoop some up.[75] Farmers were dumbfounded—"we are lost for words"[76]—but did not dare to show open hostility. In reality farmers were deeply dissatisfied but kept it bottled up.[77] Such feelings were especially strong among farmers from ethnic minorities such as the Lao Phuan and Lao Song who had migrated into the central region. They said: "these Thais are not our fathers. We are their slaves. There's no need to learn Thai so well that you can read. Just so they cannot swear at our mothers. That's enough."[78] And, "listen, I bring you up so that you don't have to be their slave".[79]

# THE PERSISTENCE OF THE SUBSISTENCE VILLAGE ECONOMY IN THE NORTH, SOUTH, AND ISAN 1855–1932

I N the central region the production system moved from subsistence towards production for sale. But until 1932 in other regions of Siam, subsistence remained the major form of production. This was most evident in Isan and less so in the south and north.

In the south and north, specialised export products developed— namely tin in the south and teak in the north. But both products were concentrated in particular areas and did not affect the village economy in general.

## 1.1 North

In the past, the north traded with Yunnan in China and Moulmein in Burma. The traders were Haw Chinese, Thai Yai (Shan), and Burmese. They used horses and mules to carry iron, opium, bronze pots, and beeswax from Yunnan, and cloth from Moulmein. In the north, they purchased salt, betelnut, and raw cotton to sell in Yunnan, and lac, ivory, and tobacco to sell in Moulmein.[1] The most important trade was floating teak down the Salween river to Moulmein.[2] At the end of the nineteenth century when more Chinese from the central region began settling in the north—from Nakhon Sawan to Tak, from Tak to Chiang Mai—a trading network extended from Chiang Mai to Bangkok. The major trade route was no longer Moulmein-Tak-Chiang Mai, but from Bangkok to Nakhon Sawan by land, and then by boat up the Ping river to Chiang Mai. In 1898, 70.5 percent of goods moving to the north used this route,[3] and it remained the major route until the railway to Chiang Mai opened in 1922. On this route there were around a thousand poled cargo boats called scorpion-tailed boats. Each boat carried 2.5 tons and took two to three months for a Chiang Mai-Bangkok-Chiang Mai round trip. Significantly, the products traded from the north were forest goods such as lac, cutch, *miang* (fermented tea), *si-siat* (styrax benzoin), ivory, opium, hides, horn, beeswax, and saltpetre. The major production good—paddy—was not traded out.[4] Another important communication route from the north down to the central region was the Nan river, from Nan down to Uttaradit or Tha Sao. Products from Nan were also forest goods, especially hides and horn, but no paddy. On the contrary, Phrae and Nan had to buy rice from Uttaradit. Goods were carried in *rua chala*, boats dug out from a large tree trunk, which travelled in groups of twenty to thirty boats.[5] Products traded out of the north at the end of the nineteenth century were still forest goods, and remained so until the railway was built to Chiang Mai in 1922.

This fact is very important because it implies that the Bowring treaty had almost no effect on the north except for the entry of foreign capital to produce and export teak from the 1880s. But teak production was controlled by foreign companies (Bombay-Burma, Borneo, East Asiatic, and Siam Forest) and by the local princes, and the labour in the teak business was Khamu. As a result, the effect on production in general was very little.[6] The opening of the country in 1855, which stimulated commercial rice production in the central region, had no equivalent impact in the north mainly because of communication difficulties. As there was no rice production for export, northern farmers had no export product to generate enough cash income to buy imports. In the period at the end of the nineteenth century which saw change at the village level in the central region, there was no change at the village level in the north. The subsistence economy clearly still operated. Outside Chiang Mai city, there was no market. In farmers' houses, there was no cash. The Chinese traders in scorpion-tail boats had to bring betel and salted *pla thu* to exchange for deer antlers, hides, and lac.[7]

In the late nineteenth and early twentieth century, the state began to collect taxes in cash. In 1873, the tax-farming system was introduced into Chiang Mai for lac, beeswax, betel, Chinese sweetmeats (*khanom chan-op*), opium, and gambling dens for example.[9] In 1900, when the administration of Chiang Mai was more completely merged in with Bangkok, the land tax was collected in cash, and also capitation tax at four baht a head for men aged eighteen to sixty. Farmers were forced to sell their produce and to enter into the capitalist system. They faced difficulty as they did not know what to sell to raise the cash for tax payment, and in many places they resisted, resulting in the Phaya Phap revolt in 1889, Nan revolt in 1902, Phrae Ngieo revolt in 1902, and Phrao revolt in 1902.[10]

Change came when the railway was built to the north, reaching Lampang in 1916 and Chiang Mai in 1922. Rice began to be produced for export to Bangkok. A rice mill was built near the Chiang Mai railway station.[11] In 1925 an estimated 650,000 *hap* of rice was sent from Chiang Mai to Bangkok, equivalent to 5 percent of total overseas rice exports. In 1935, the amount increased to 1.3 million *hap* or 9 percent of total rice exports.[12] Of this total, 35 percent was sent from Chiang Mai as milled rice.[13] This means that the trend of commercial rice production in the north began from the 1920s onwards. At the rural level, the immediate result of this change was that northern princes and Chinese claimed and developed land. Some princes had begun earlier from the end of the nineteenth and start of the twentieth century. They used the device of seizing land for free. Sometimes they took elephants to rampage on the land and prevent villagers cultivating, or they spread tales that certain villagers were ghouls (living dead) to scare their neighbours to flee.[14] Chinese invested in dikes and then laid claim to the land so developed. The state accepted these claims. Chinese built dikes at Mae Rim, Mae Taeng, Sansai, and Chomthong. Northern princes built dikes at Sanpatong, Chomthong, and Mae Taeng.[15] Villagers who had no land either became tenants or migrated northwards to Fang, Phan, and Chiang Saen to take up new land.[16] In 1930 Zimmerman's survey found that 27 percent of farming families in the north were landless.[17] The north had limited valley land in the sparse and narrow areas between the hills. Villagers could not expand outward very far. Hence only a few years after the start of commercial rice production the problem of landlessness appeared. The process of princes and Chinese becoming landowners as state ownership of property weakened, followed the same pattern as in the central plain, only fifty years behind. Similarly, high-interest moneylending which in the central plain made farmers lose land placed on mortgage, also began in the valley around Chiang Mai. Again the lenders were mostly general goods traders. Examples of big moneylending families were Chutima, Nimmanhemin, and Wibunsanti.[18]

Once rice could be sold, farmers bought clothing for wearing outside the home but still used home-woven inside the house. They also began to use kerosene oil in place of pig fat or *yang* oil, matches in place of flint, and used imported metal bars instead of ore dug from the hills to beat into knives, machetes, hoes, and spades.[19]

However, by 1932 the process of change from subsistence to commercial economy had run for only ten years and only around Chiang Mai. The northern region as a whole was still a subsistence economy. Professor Zimmerman who surveyed the northern region economy in 1930 wrote clearly that villagers grew rice primarily for their own consumption, and grew vegetables, tobacco, and cotton for their own use. Similarly, under every house he found a loom, and saw that villagers still wove for themselves. Surplus rice was exchanged for other articles such as salt.[20] In 1917 villagers around Chiang Mai still spun their own cotton yarn.[21] Weaving for own use in Nan and around Chiang Mai only ceased at the end of the Second World War.[22] In certain places like amphoe Mae Chaem, Chiang Mai, weaving for own use continues to the present.[23] In the central plain, places where home-weaving survived to the Second World War were the exception, but among ethnic minority villages in the north they remained the rule. Similarly, other old activities continued. At the end of the war, the use of hired labour had not surfaced in some areas.[24] People still used exchange labour. At amphoe Sansai near Chiang Mai, pounding rice ceased only ten years ago.[25]

## 4.2 South

Before the Bowring treaty, there was trading in the south but it was state monopoly trading in which the provincial governors (*chao muang*) acted as agents. The important goods were tin, birds nests, and forest goods such as wood, ivory, and hides. After the Bowring treaty, the monopoly trading system was cancelled. Trade in tin and forest goods continued in parallel with subsistence production. Forest goods included hides, *yang* oil, deer antlers, honey, rattan, and dried coconut. In the past villagers sieved for tin in the surface soil close to the rivers and sea coast, and sold the mineral ore to Chinese smelters who sold on to Penang and Singapore.[26] After the Bowring treaty, in the south as in the north the exports were not rice but specialised products, namely tin and the forest goods which had been exported for a long time. Particularly the western part of the southern region produced mainly tin and did not grow enough paddy. Rice was purchased from Saiburi and Marit[27] rather than from the rice-growing tracts to the east because of the difficulty of transport across the hills. Statistics of exports from four southern *monthon*—Phuket, Nakhon Sithammarat, Pattani, and Chumphon— show that all through the later Fifth Reign and the Sixth Reign, three-quarters of exports from the south came from Phuket, namely tin.[28] In 1925 southern exports (48.1 million baht) were 24 percent of total country exports (203.5 million baht).[29] As with teak production in the north, tin production did not affect the village community. From the early twentieth century, tin production used modern technology of dredges (first in 1907) and mining pumps. The investment capital was European and Chinese. The labourers were Chinese who flowed in from Singapore and Penang. Village labour was not used. Thai villagers only sieved a little ore from the water courses as they had in the past. They played no part in the boom of tin production.[30] From her study of the history of the southern tin industry, Phanni Uansakun concluded that the south had a dualistic economy. She pointed out that from the early twentieth century, large towns which produced and sold tin emerged in the western part of the region (such as Ranong, Phuket) and

Hat Yai, while the rural village communities in Surat Thani, Nakhon Sithammarat, Songkhla, and Pattani scarcely changed from before.[31]

The east of the southern region was, like the northern region, the home of Thai rice-growing villagers. The Bowring treaty and opening of the country in 1855 had almost no effect on these farmers. At Phatthalung in 1889 King Chulalongkorn wrote an account of the rural economy of the south: "Local people here have a tendency to be satisfied with what they have. Most of them are the same, easily content. They are not good at buying and selling. They just cultivate enough paddy to exchange with the townspeople in Songkhla for other things to eat. They weave their own clothes (*phanung*), two pieces a head a year. They do no trading but they can still live and be happy. Trading is hardly anything, except for a small amount of forest produce."[32] Prince Dilok Nopparat wrote in his thesis in 1907: "The south on the Malaysian peninsula has very little paddy cultivation."[33] Rice was occasionally transported by sailboat to sell in Malaya, but the geography of the eastern side is a narrow coastal plain (though broader than on the western side) where rice cultivation has little room to expand. "The paddy land is small and cannot be expanded because of the natural constraint."[34] Even the building of the railway in 1922 from Bangkok to the southern border at Pair for onward connection to Penang, did not result in rice being transported for sale in Bangkok, only import of clothing and other articles from Bangkok to the south.[35]

From the 1920s to the Second World War, rice production increased in the broad plain around Nakhon Sithammarat and Phatthalung, especially in amphoes Pak Phanang, Hua Sai, and Chian Yai. Many rice mills appeared, especially at Pak Phanang,[36] Nakhon Sithammarat, and Songkhla, and rice was sold to Malaya. The pattern found in the central region and the north, whereby the nobles with influence laid claims to land through bureaucratic power, began to surface but in a much more limited area. For example, Khun Phibun Prempradit in amphoe Phibun, Nakhon Sithammarat, and Khun Ruksa Saiburi in amphoe Tha Sala, Nakhon Sithammarat, were both *kamnan* (village heads) who laid claim to lots of land. Khun Phibun used corvée labour to build a dike at Wang

Tong to enable the land he had claimed to produce more rice.[37] Many people moved in to be tenants. The case was similar to that of Phra-klaklangsomon who claimed land in amphoe Kao Lieo, Nakhon Sawan. In addition, local Malay nobles claimed a lot of land during the period when private property rights were emerging. For example the family of Pin-tamma-ngong, ruler of Satun, acquired a lot of land in Satun.[38] Examples also appeared of land acquired through moneylending such as the Thirawat and Sethapakdi families in Surat Thani.[39] Professor Zimmerman gave figures that in 1930, landless families were 14 percent of all farming families in the south.[40]

During the 1920s, some fruits such as mangosteen and durian began to be sent by rail for sale in Bangkok.[41]

In the future, rubber planting would be an important change in the rural south. But before the Second World War, it was still of little importance. Rubber was only 2 percent of total country exports in 1930–34.[42] The area planted increased gradually from around 100,000 *rai* in the period 1899–1917 to 778,000 *rai* in 1928.[43] Rubber plantations were widespread in Trang. The owners of large plantations were officials and Chinese traders, not villagers. Examples include Phraya Rasdanu Pradit (Kosimpi Na Ranong), Luang Sophonphlarak (Tiang Hui Susaha), Captain Hall (Nilpradup family), and Dek Chuan.[44] Villagers took up rubber planting after the officials and Chinese, but only in small plots of up to ten *rai*.[45] Rubber planting gave farmers more labouring work. After the rice season, farmers would find temporary work as rubber tappers on big plantations.[46]

Even though these changes emerged, in 1932 the village community in the south was still at base a subsistence economy. Professor Zimmerman reported that in 1930 only 20 percent of rice produced in the south was exported for sale.[47] Weaving for home use was still widespread. In many localities in Trang, weaving ceased only twenty years ago.[48] In amphoe Chaiya, Surat Thani, weaving for home use was abandoned during the Second World War.[49] Exchange labour ceased only recently. For example, in amphoe Yanthakhao, Trang, exchange labour disappeared only twenty years ago.[50] In Surat Thani the *chang wan* (ask the artisan for a favour) system remains even today; in the event of a death, neighbours help out to make the coffin for free. Previously neighbours helped out also in house building without charging for their labour (*long khaek ban*).[51] Pounding rice for own use ceased only twenty to forty years ago.[52]

## 4.3 Isan

Isan is the region where the village subsistence economy persisted to the greatest extent. In some localities, subsistence style production continues even today, such as around Sakon Nakhon and Nakhon Phanom beyond the Phuphan range where every household still weaves in the space under the house. In Ban Nawa Tai, amphoe Phosai, Ubon Ratchathani, cloth is still woven for own use and spinning ceased only ten years ago.[53] In amphoe Dong Luang, Nakhon Phanom, they still spin and weave. On the route from amphoe Kalasin to amphoe Kuchinarai in Kalasin, every village household has a loom for weaving cloth for own use. Even in central Isan in Mahasarakham, some villages such as Nong Khoen Chang in amphoe Muang still spin and weave. Pounding rice for own use still relies on female and child labour three times a day, for example at Ban Nawa Tai. Old-style metalworking using village bellows survives to the present, and there are regular village smiths (who are also farmers), for example at tambon Dong Luang, Nakhon Phanom and amphoes Phosai and Khemmarat in Ubon Ratchathani.

Trading in Isan was solely in forest produce. Originally it was for *suai* tax. But when tax collection changed to cash at the end of the Fifth Reign, villagers sold forest produce to raise the cash to pay the four-baht poll tax. As Isan has no important water transport, before the coming of the railway, long-distance trade relied on carts and human porterage. The long-distance traders in early Isan were the Kula. They generally only brought goods out for sale, and purchased nothing for the return trip. Later, Chinese traders came to buy forest goods such as dried ox and buffalo hides, ox and buffalo bones, ivory, rattan, and castor seeds. They moved the goods by cart or porterage to Korat, and from there by porterage along the difficult passage over the Dongphayayen to Bangkok.[54] Because there was little trade in Isan, poll tax collection created great difficulties for the villagers: "finding four baht was very tough". Sometimes villagers had to sell their cattle.[55] Tax collection in cash forced the villages into the capitalist system, making them find something to sell against their own wishes. The Bowring treaty and the opening of the country to free trade had no effect on Isan. Isan had no export goods specific to the region equivalent to the teak in the north or tin in the south.

Some change occurred when Bangkok built the railway across the Dongphayayen to Korat in 1900.[56] Chinese went to settle in Isan, but many fewer than in the central region. They were concentrated in Korat, and gradually expanded to other important provinces—Roi-et, Buriram, Surin, and Ubon Ratchathani—where they were concentrated in the provincial towns. Only later did they reach Khon Kaen, Phu Khieo, Udon Thani, Loei, and Sakon Nakhon.[57] The railway across the Dongphayayen stimulated commercial rice production in the tract around Korat and some adjacent areas. Rice was carried by boat and cart to store in Korat then transported by rail for sale in Bangkok. Later when the railway expanded to Buriram (1925), Surin (1926), and Ubon Ratchathani (1930), Chinese traders established rice depots close to the railway stations. Korat became the consolidating market for rice, with granaries where rice could be stored while waiting for a good price before forwarding by rail to Bangkok. Rice mills were established in several places.[58] In 1930 there were thirty-three in Isan, with thirteen at Korat, five at Ubon, five at Khukhan, four at Surin, three at Khon Kaen, two at Buriram, and one at Roi-et.[59] Commercial rice production expanded in southern Isan following the railway, but in the centre and north of the region there was no impact, as can be seen from an official document which noted: "the rice market is at Korat. But people from Udon cannot sell there because the communications are not convenient. The rice price is not enough to cover transport costs."[60] Because Isan is a big region with one-third of the land area and population of the country at that time, there was still land available for expansion of production.[61] In 1925 rice exports from Isan were 1,700,000 *hap* (102,816 tons), equal to 7 percent of total country rice exports. In 1935, the proportion increased to 18 percent.[62] Once rice was exported, foreign imports entered including clothing, kerosene, and aluminium goods. Around Korat, weaving diminished. Transport across the Dongphayayen by cart, elephant, and human porters disappeared.[63]

However, change took place only along the railway line and most especially at Korat. Far out in the villages, the situation remained almost unchanged from the past. There were no nobles and Chinese capitalists competing to come and control the land by building dikes or digging canals to develop the land. And there were no cases of moneylenders. Besides, apart from rice, no other commercial crops were developed, and the land was not very suitable for rice as it was saline and not water-retentive. When Prince Damrong went to inspect monthons Udon and Isan in 1906, he reported on the state of the Isan village at the start of this century in a most interesting way:

> Since entering monthon Udon, I have visited many villages along the way. Some places have large villages established for a long time over many generations. I went down to ask about the social customs of these villagers. From the villagers' replies, I found one surprising fact. Each village household has a house with enough space for living and a granary to store enough rice for one year. In the yard of the house they plant chilli, eggplant, galangal, and lemongrass for making curry. Outside the house they have a garden for fruits such as banana, sugarcane, betel, and coconut. And between the garden and the paddy field, there is a space to plant mulberry for raising silkworms. Each household has enough paddy fields and cattle to grow enough rice for the whole household. In the rice-growing season, everyone helps—man and woman, child and adult. After the season, men travel to find things to sell. Women stay at home, raise silk, and weave cloth. Leftover food is used to raise chicken and pigs for sale. Villagers around here make all their own food and scarcely have to buy a single thing. The things they have to buy are metal articles like hoes, spades, and knives; and crockery. Sometimes they buy yarn for weaving,

or cloth and other attractive things brought by traders. They have just enough cash for these purchases because their cattle have surplus young, and they raise extra pigs and chickens with surplus food from each meal. These animals can be sold for cash to buy what they want. Each family is independent. Nobody is slave and nobody master. Family members are under the guardianship of the head of their family, and in addition there is a *phuyaiban* (village headman) and *kamnan* (sub-district head) to oversee. They administer themselves easily. But in the whole *tambon* (sub-district) it is impossible to find one rich man with 200 baht or more stored away. Yet you cannot find a single person who is poor to the point of being another's servant. They must have been like this for a hundred years. Because the villagers can farm to feed themselves without resorting to cash, the feeling that they need cash is not strong. Money does not have the same power as in the city which is called "civilised". So nobody accumulates but you cannot call them poor because they feed themselves happily and contentedly. I conveyed this information to Dr Braddock and asked him whether foreigners would think this community was happy or sad. Dr Braddock, who is an American, answered that the socialists who make trouble in Western countries would like to be just like these villagers. In reality the sort of society which the socialists desire has existed in this country for hundreds and thousands of years. Like the proverb: "nothing new in the world".[64]

The penetration of central power and the capitalist system triggered the greatest resistance in Isan, because state and capitalism clashed with a village which was rather independent. Professor James C. Scott states that peasant revolts happen when trade and state intrude into an area where the peasant community has high social cohesion.[65] Peasant revolts appeared often in Isan. The most important instance was the holy man revolt of 1901–2, which covered the whole region, followed by the Nong Mak Kaeo holy man revolt in 1924, and the Mo Lamnoichada revolt in 1936. As late as 1959 there was the Sila Wongsin revolt. Holy men appeared regularly in Isan, promising to bring back the world of the primordial socialism of the village community.[66] Other regions had peasant revolts opposing the inroads of the state and capitalism, such as the Phaya Phap revolt in 1889[67] and the Ngieo revolt in Phrae in 1902 in the north;[68] the Phaya Khaek Chet Hua Muang (Seven Provinces) revolt in 1902[69] and the Phu Wiset revolt in 1909–10 in the south.[70] But the Isan peasant revolts covered the widest area and were the strongest. These various revolts show that the village community in Siam outside the central region tried to maintain its own style of internal self-government and village subsistence. Because villages had strong internal bonds, these small communities resisted the inroads of the state and capitalism. They did not welcome capitalism as is often understood. The Isan village communities had their uniqueness and the highest internal cohesion, hence they resisted the most fully, in contrast to the central region where the entry of capitalism did not provoke the same result.

These revolts also show that villagers' resistance took the form of the village resisting the state, not tenants against a landlord class.[71]

The belief in ancestor spirits which is the ideological structure of kin-based society persisted strongly in Isan. The spread of Buddhism was much slower than in the central region. When Phra Achan Fan Acharo travelled to preach *thamma* in Isan in 1929, he had to compromise with the village spirits in Khon Kaen. Before preaching a sermon he told the villagers "Me and the local spirits can live together.... I'm like their grandson."[72] The Buddhism that appeared in Isan had a local flavour. It concentrated on meditation practice by individuals or small communities more than on the religious organisation and monkhood. In Isan Buddhism, there were *mo thamma*, local teachers who were not monks but who propagated religion and performed ceremonies in place of monks.[73] At the same time, belief in spirits survived in the village. Spirit medium rituals were a permanent feature, and mediums were found everywhere. Some villagers entered the monkhood but afterwards returned to spirit belief again.[74] Belief in spirits was very strong in the village community of minorities such as the Kha and So in Sakon Nakhon,[75] and the Suai in Sisaket.[76] In these places there is no belief in Buddhism even today. Some minority settlements have a Buddhist *wat*, but they are deserted and the monks have all fled because the villagers did not give support to the *wat*. Spirit priests still have the highest power in the commmunity.[77] In minority communities in other regions, spirit belief is similarly strong, such as among the Lawa in Nan who still believe in lineage spirits who descend through the strict maternal bloodline.[78] The Lao Song community in the central region still upholds belief in both Buddhism and spirits. Merit offerings are offered to the spirits first before giving to the monks.[79] Phra Srithammanusat, the elderly abbot of Wat Suriyawong in Ratchaburi town, related that in his experience: "teaching people to give up spirits is difficult. In the time of my youth, the people believed in the spirits of the sky and of every bend in the river. The temple follows the villagers. Villagers believe so much in ancestor spirits. It still exists now ... they mix them all up."[80]

# CHAPTER FIVE

# CONCLUSION

THE Thai village economy in the past was a subsistence economy. Production for food and for own use persisted and could be reproduced without reliance on the outside world. Bonds within the village were strong. Control of land was mediated by membership of the community. Cooperative exchange labour was used in production. Individual families were self-sufficient. Agriculture and artisan work—that is, rice cultivation and weaving—were combined in the same household. Beliefs were held in common, namely belief in the spirits of the common ancestors of the village. Kinship links were maintained. People cooperated in social activities and there was no class division, except for the existence of slaves who were accepted as a part of the family. There was no class conflict within the village. Production relations were similar to those of the primordial socialist community—a small community in which people help one another in a spirit of common humanity. But the production technology of the community was low. Finding food directly from nature (by fishing, collecting vegetables, growing rain-fed paddy), weaving, and gathering forest produce—all were dependent on the plentifulness of nature because the tools used were old-fashioned. Production was only enough for subsistence with almost no surplus. If there was drought or flood, there was not enough to eat.

Historical changes originated from outside the village. The development of the state, and later of capitalism, were both located outside the village. State and capitalism affected life in the village, but neither state nor capitalism was an institution of the villagers. State and capitalism did not come to develop the village, only to extract benefit from the villagers. As a result, the villagers did not cooperate wholeheartedly with these two institutions. The villagers were dragged into cooperation, and in reality they resisted state and capitalism throughout, both silently and openly. Production for food and own use—cultivating rice for home consumption, weaving local-style cloth, pounding rice, not using hired labour—was sustained over a long period. Many believe that villagers were happy to enter into capitalism but the reality was the opposite. The villagers' resistance shows that they were conscious that state and capitalism were foreign and unnatural. They were not happy to cooperate. Their institution was the village. The process of domination of the villagers' consciousness from outside was incomplete. There was a gap. The village consciousness remained independent. The community consciousness of ethnic minorities survived in the Thai countryside. State and capitalism faced resistance at the level of consciousness as well.

But villagers fought back in old ways. They had no strategy. They did not adjust. They did not change their productive power and technology.

Three things worked against change: first, the sheer abundance of the natural resources available in the past; second, the security provided by the village community; and third, the special nature of the Thai state and capitalism.

On the first point, Siam in the past had such plentiful natural resources, especially reserves of unused land with relatively high fertility. Villagers could draw on these natural resources to make up for the backwardness of their technology, and also to make up for the exploitation by state and capitalism. As a result, villagers could fight back for a long time on the foundations of the old production system. The village did not disintegrate easily because it had a strong basis of natural resources as a cushion.

On the second point, the system of village society was good. Members shared mutual sympathy and cooperation which gave them security and contentment. The institution of the village sustained them throughout.

As a result, the villagers had no motivation to change, to seek a new system, to make any long-term plan to solve their problems. The system of village community had its good side, but this good side was at the same time a bad side because it closed the villagers off and failed to stimulate a search to develop or find new ways to fight.

On the third point, state and capitalism extracted surplus directly from the village by force rather than through the economic mechanism. This retarded the development of other classes between state and village, and deprived the village of the leadership of a reforming landlord class or progressive bourgeoisie.

The old Thai state extracted labour services and produce taxes directly from the village. This was different from the experience in European history where exploitation in society was exploitation of individual by individual, for example, of the peasant by the landlord. In that case, the landlords intervened to manage the village production and improve it to some extent. The old Thai state was not an organisation involved in production, only in taxation. It had no thought of nurturing the village at all. Besides, the old Thai state blocked the rise of a free bourgeoisie which might have provided leadership for the villagers' struggle, as occurred in the European experience. The Thai state limited any development at the provincial level by coopting provincial leaders completely onto the side of the state. It did not support and sometimes suppressed any collaboration at the regional level which the centre did not accept. As a result, regional towns were not independent and not important. In Thai history, there were only two lead characters, the institutions of state and village. All other parts were supporting roles.

Thai capitalism was not independent from the state but depended on the monopoly power of the state. This was clearly apparent in the system of tax farmers who squeezed surplus from the villages outside the economic mechanism, and who resolutely extracted exploitative interest and rentals from the villagers both through trickery and through the power of local influence. The tax farmers accepted the ideology of the sakdina state and acted as if they were the state in their dealings with the village. They extracted tax from the countryside by squeezing the old production system, the sakdina production system, rather than generating a surplus through modernising agriculture or founding industries. This parasitic capitalism arose in other Third World countries too.

Even when capitalism developed, it was not in line with changes in the village community. Capitalism arose outside Thailand and spread into the country, impacting on the village in its old form, with no change in the structure of production or technology, no development of private property rights in land, and no strong growth of a local bourgeoisie. Capitalism collided with the old village community. The village had to fight back, even using old methods which put it at a big disadvantage. The case was different from the European experience where the village changed by stages over a long historical period from ancient to modern times. When the capitalist system emerged, private property rights had already developed, agriculture had passed through a revolution, and the buds of a local bourgeois class were already strong.

The old-style village community with no technological development could not fight back against state and capital. But the village did not disintegrate as in Latin America but kept up the struggle for a long time. The abundance of natural resources served as a counterweight. But later, population increased, resources were over-used, and this natural abundance dwindled. The problems inherent in fighting back in old ways—problems which in reality had always been there over a long time—now became apparent. The village was in decline. The number of landless increased continuously. Villagers were confused because the institutions important to their lives were breaking apart with nothing to replace them. The problem for the future is: how to preserve the good aspects of the village community—how to preserve the old-style production relations, but improve the form and increase the productive power by developing the technology in the village. This will enable the villagers to retain their uniqueness and commitment, to develop their organisational strength to increase their bargaining power, and to provide the poor with some institutional support they can rely on. State and capitalism should not see themselves as separate from the village. In reality, state, capitalism, and village exist in the same Thai society, in the same system, and must depend on one another. Allowing one part to decline while others prosper by exploiting the part in decline, will not generate true prosperity, will not create stability in Thai society, and will not make the Thai people content.

# NOTES

## CHAPTER ONE

1. Tadayo Watabe, "The Development of Rice Cultivation," in *Thailand: A Rice-Growing Society*, ed. Yoneo Ishii (Honolulu: University of Hawaii Press, 1978), 3–14; interview C:33.

2. Interview N:69.

3. Bunchuai Srisawat, *Thai sipsongpanna* [The Thai of Sipsongpanna] (Bangkok: 1955); Jogendra Nath Phukan, "The Economic History of Assam under the Ahoms," Ph.D. thesis, Gauhati University, 1973.

4. Phuankham Tuikieo, comp., *Phongsawadan muang chiang rung* [Chiang Rung chronicle], typescript 23 February 1981, 69.

5. W.C. Dodd, *The Tai Race: Elder Brother of the Chinese* (Cedar Rapids: Torch Press, 1923), 24.

6. Jit Phumisak, *Khwam pen ma khong kham sayam thai lao lae khom lae laksana thang sangkhom khong chu chonchat* [Etymology of the terms Siam, Thai, Lao, and Khom and the social characteristics of nationalities] (Bangkok: Krungsayam, 1976), 245; *Nangsu huang chieo bun hien thong khao* vol. 34, pp. 40–1, compiled during the Tai-seng dynasty, equivalent to 1777, Thonburi, translated by Khun Chen Chin-akson (Sutchai), states similarly that "seasons in Siam are variable. The land is flooded. People must live in tall houses," published in *Chotmaihet ruang phraratchamaitri nai rawang krung sayam kap krung chin* [Documents concerning relations between Siam and China] (Bangkok: Phiphanthanakon, 1933); Ishii, "History and Rice-Growing," in *Thailand*, ed. Ishii.

7. Interview I:168, N:71

8. James McCarthy, *Surveying and Exploring in Siam* (London: John Murray, 1900), 43

9. See fn. 8; Khun Rattanawetchasakha, "Prapheni lae khwampen yu bang prakan khong chao changwat lanchang" [Some points on life and customs of Lanchang province], radio broadcast 25 August 1941, National Archives SP 4/21; interview S:97

10. Khun Rattanawetchasakha, "Prapheni"; interview N:71 with Tit Tankai, a Thin, who claimed his people moved every six years.

11. See fn. 8; Thawat Buntok, "Prawatisat sangkhom isan tai tang tae samai ayutthaya tung rattanakosin ton ton" [The history of southern Isan society from the Ayutthaya period to early Rattanakosin], papers of the conference on history and culture of southern Isan, Buriram Teachers College, 22–4 November 1982; Thawat stated that the Kha, Lawa, Lua, Kui, and Suai are the same ethnic group with similar language, culture, beliefs, and customs.

12. Charles Gutzlaff, *Journal of Two Voyages along the Coast of China in 1831 and 1832* (New York: John P. Haven, 1833), 38; interview I:136 with Mrs Taem Than-ngam, a Suai, who stated that the Suai had no religion and no state.

13. Robert Lingat, *Prawatisat gotmai thai* [History of Thai laws] (Bangkok: Thammasat University, 1940); Lingat refers to E. Diguet, "Etude de la langue tai".

14. Jit Phumisak (Somsamai Srisudravarna), *Chomna sakdina thai* [The real face of Thai sakdina] (Bangkok: Chakranukul, 1974), 111–27.

15. Georges Condominas, *From Lawa to Mon, from Saa' to Thai* (Canberra: Australian National University, 1990), 56–7.

16. Shigeharu Tanabe, "Guardian Spirit Cults of the Tai Lu in Yunan and the Socialist Transformation," mimeo draft, 1983, 3.

17. Interview I:148; Fong Sithitham, "Silpa-watthanatham ariya prapheni khong di boran" [Art, culture, customs: good things from the past], Thai Isan Ban Hao [Thai-Isan our home], exhibition on Isan culture, Ubon Ratchathani Teachers College, 5–9 December 1977, (Ubon Ratchathani: Padungsan, 1977), 146.

18. Chatthip Nartsupha, and Pranut Sapphayasan, "Udomkan khabot phu mi bun isan" [Ideology of Isan millenarian revolts], in *Khwam chua phra si-an*

*lae khabot phu mi bun nai sangkhom thai* [Millenarian beliefs and revolts in Thai society], eds. Phornphen Hantrakun and Atcharaphon Kamutphitsamai (Bangkok: Sangsan, 1984).

19. Condominas, *From Lawa*.

20. See below.

21. Robert Lingat, *Prawatisat*, 8; Keo Mannivanna believes the phrase "lord of life" originates from the Lao king repriving hill and forest peoples captured in warfare, see Keo Mannivanna, "Aspects socio-economiques du Laos medieval," in Centre d'Etudes et de Recherches Marxists, *Sur le Mode de Production Asiatic* (Paris: Editions Sociales, 1974), 309–25.

22. Phukan, "Economic History".

23. Tanabe, "Guardian Spirit Cults".

24. Interview N:69

25. Prasoet na Nakhon (trans.), *Mangraisat* [The law of Mengrai] (Bangkok: Srinakharintharawirot University, 1978), 110; Chusit Chuchat, "Kan phalit phua liang tua eng nai sangkhom sakdina: suksa chapho kan phalit radap mu ban nai phak nua khong prathet thai pho. so. 1839–2475" [Subsistence production in sakdina society; study of village production in the north, 1296–1932], undated typescript.

26. Withit Sujjapong, "A Preliminary Study on Economic History of Modern Thailand," M. Econ. thesis, Hitotsubashi University, 1980; Yuk Sriariya, *Withi kan phalit thai boran* [The ancient Thai mode of production] (1983).

27. Sukhothai Inscription 49 includes the passage: "Nai Sornsak asked the king for forest to convert to paddy... the king ordered him to turn a thousand *rai* of forest into paddy to give to the temple." *Prachum silacharuk phak thi 3* [Collected inscriptions, part 3] (Bangkok: Prime Minister's Office, 1964).

28. Phra aiyakan bet set matra 52 [Miscellaneous laws, clause 52], *Kotmai tra sam duang* [Three Seals Code] (Bangkok: Khurusapha, 1962).

29. Miscellaneous laws clause 54, in *Kotmai tra sam duang*.

30. Phra ratchakamnot kao thi 44 [Old decrees no. 44], in *Kotmai tra sam duang*

31. Miscellaneous laws clause 65, in *Kotmai tra sam duang*.

32. Nicolas Gervaise, *The Natural and Political History of the Kingdom of Siam*, trans. and ed. John Villiers (Bangkok: White Lotus, 1998), 98.

33. Lingat, *Prawatisat*, 13–32.

34. Civil hierarchy law and military hierarchy law in *Kotmai tra sam duang.*

35. John Crawfurd, *Journal of an Embassy from the Governor-General of India to the Courts of Siam and Cochin China* (London: Henry Colburn, 1828; reprint Kuala Lumpur: Oxford University Press, 1967).

36. Wachirayan Archive R.4, J.S. 1222 No 117, royal command about the law on the grant of house, land, paddy-field, orchard, 7 April ro. so. 80 (1861).

37. Announcement of the ministry of public works 13 January 1891, cited by Lingat, *Prawatisat*, 79.

38. Dilok, Prinz von Siam, *Landwirtschaft in Siam* (Leipzig: Verlag von C. L. Hirschfeld, 1908), chapter 3.

39. Report of the committee scrutinising the economic plan, 12 March 1933, appendix B in *Pridi phanomyong kap sangkhom thai* [Pridi Banomyong and Thai society] (Bangkok: Thammasat University, 1983), 266.

40. Lingat, *Prawatisat*, 81–2. In the old law there was no term to refer to people's rights in land. The phrase "property right" (*kammasit*) was used in law in the modern sense for the first time in the proclamation on claiming land under the Prawet Burirom canal and its offshoots, 1898, clause 17, and in court decisions one to two years earlier; see Lingat, *Prawatisat*, 31. From the Ayutthaya period, the old title deed (*chanot*) conveyed no meaning of property right but recorded the land occupant's obligation to pay tax. Lingat, *Prawatisat*, 24. The land title deed became a proof of land ownership in the proclamation on land titles, 15 September 1901, of which clause 6 stated: "The owner of the land covered by this title deed has property right." *Prachum kotmai prachamsok* [Collected laws of the period], vol 18, cited in Sunthari Asawai, *Botbat khong ratthaban lae ekkachon nai kan phatthana: phicharana chapho korani prawat khrongkan rangsit pho. so. 2431 thung 2457* [Government and private roles in development: study of the Rangsit project 1888–1914] (Bangkok: Thai Studies Institute, Thammasat University, 1977), 110–1; however the system of property rights was not yet secure because there were conflicting interpretations until 1934.

41. New decrees clause 12, in *Kotmai tra sam duang*, vol 5, 237–42. Reduction of corvée from six to four months was announced on 24 October 1785, and from four to three months on 13 April 1810, see Sathien Lailak, *Prachum kotmai prachamsok* [Collected laws of the period], vol 4 (Bangkok: Daily Mail, 1935), 7.

42. The law required payment of rice tax at two *thang* per *rai*. This law was issued in the Third Reign, indicating that during the first two reigns tax was collected in rice not cash, using the rate under the old law of two *thang* (*thang*=20 litres) per *rai*. Farmers had to deliver the rice to the royal granary themselves, and were forced to buy back two *thang* per *rai* rice from the royal granary at four *at* (*at*=1/64th of a baht) per *thang*. This law changed to collection in cash at the rate of one *salung* one *fuang* (*salung*=1/4 baht, *fuang*=1/8 baht) per *rai*. For the tax on forest produce, see Bunrot Kaeokanha, "Kan kep suai nai samai rattanakosin ton ton (pho. so. 2324–2422)" [Tax collection in early Rattanakosin, 1781–1868], M.A. thesis, Chulalongkorn University, 1975.

43. David Joel Steinberg, *In Search of Southeast Asia: A Modern History* (New York: Praeger, 1971), 112.

44. Chusit Chuchat, "Wiwatthanakan sethakit muban nai phak nua khong prathet thai pho. so. 2394–2475" [Development of the village economy in northern Thailand 1851–1932], M.A. thesis, Srinakharintharawirot University, 1980, chapter 4.

45. Interview with Achan Surasing Samruam Chimphanao, Chiang Rai Teachers College, 29 December 1981. According to the local legend recorded in Thai Yuan script, grandmother and grandfather Sae were the ancestral spirits of the Lua. Today villagers in tambons Suthep, Mae Hia, and Doi Kham, amphoe Muang, Chiang Mai still make offerings every year in the ninth month. See footnote 29 in Arunrat Wichiankhieo, "Kan wikhro sangkhom chiangmai samai rattanakosin ton ton tam ton chabap bailan phak nua" [Analysis of Chiangmai society in the Rattanakosin period according to the northern palm leaf manuscripts], M.A. thesis, Chulalongkorn University, 1977, 268; *Tamnan phun muang chiangmai* [Local Chiang Mai legends] (Bangkok: Prime Minister's Office, 1971), 111; Chalatchai Ramitanon, "Prapheni kan song phi chao nai lae botbat thang sangkhom: korani suksa nai changwat chiangmai" [Customs of spirit worship and their social role: a study in Chiang Mai], research papers

of the Social Science Association annual general meeting, 24–6 July 1983; Sanguan Chotisukharat, *Prapheni thai phak nua* [Northern Thai customs] (Bangkok: Odeon Store, 1969); Kiti Kaenchampi, "Khwam chua ruang phi pu sae ya sae" [Belief in grandfather and grandmother Sae], *Suksasan* X:2–4, October 1981–September 1982; the legend of Chaophraya Ravi, which refers to a giant named Arayaka who must be worshipped with human sacrifice, has a similar theme of meeting with the Buddha and having to change the article of sacrifice. Kaeo Kanthiya read the legend from palm leaf manuscript in the temple at old Muang Klang (hamlet 10, amphoe Chomthong, Chiang Mai), see "Prawat muban muang klang" [History of Klang villages], report by Phiphat Engsin to Achan Yupin Khemmuk, history department, Chiang Mai University, 1982.

46. Mgr. J. B. Pallegoix, *Description du Royaume Thai ou Siam* (Paris, 1854) ed. M. Dassé (Bangkok: D.K Bookhouse, 1976), 118.

47. For comparison of the Asiatic and feudal modes of production, see Maurice Godelier, *The Concept of the "Asiatic Mode of Production" and Marxist Models of Social Evolution* (London: Frank Cass, 1978); Emil Oestereicher, "Marx's Comparative Historical Sociology," *Dialectical Anthropology* III:2 (May 1978).

# CHAPTER TWO

1. Subsistence production is one branch of agriculture, consisting of villagers whose main object is to produce to meet the food consumption needs of the family rather than to sell. It is production whose principle is to create use value, but which may also have some production to create exchange value as a minor objective; see Shigeharu Tanabe, "Peasant Farming Systems in Thailand: A Comparative Study of Rice Cultivation and Agricultural Technology in Chiang Mai and Ayutthaya," Ph.D. thesis, School of Oriental and African Studies, University of London, 1981. Interviews with villagers give a consistent picture of the Thai village economy before 1855 as a subsistence economy, which I shall show is in line with the report of the social survey by Professor Carle C. Zimmerman who stated that up to 1931 the economies of Isan and the

south were still subsistence economies; see Zimmerman, *Siam: Rural Economic Survey, 1930–31* (Bangkok: Bangkok Times, 1931), 199; and also in line with the work of the Dutch engineer, J. Homan van der Heide, "The Economical Development of Siam during the Last Half Century," *Journal of the Siam Society* 3, 1906, 77–80. Charuwan Thammawat, a scholar of Thai literature, stated similarly that the ancient Thai economy had the nature of subsistence, see "Sethasat chak wannakam isan" [Economics from Isan literature], papers from the Thai Studies Conference 10–11 January 1983. Charuwan points to the mention of subsistence economy in literature as follows: "*Phun khun bu homratchathirat*", "Phraya Khamkong teaching his *phrai*", "Poems of Withun Banthit", "Poems of the grandfather teaching his grandchildren", "Inthiyan teaching his children".

2. Interview S:113.

3. Interview I:132.

4. Interview C:25.

5. Interview I:144.

6. Interview I:179.

7. Interview S:113.

8. Interview C:24.

9. From a verse in Mallika Kananurak, *Phleng klom dek thai muslim phak tai* [Thai-Muslim children's music from the south] (Pattani: Songkhla Nakharin College, n.d.), 26.

10. National Archives R.5 M.2 12 K/1 Ratchawong Ratchabut Luang Siworarat (amphoe Phonphisai, Nong Khai) to the court jury, 26 May 1887.

11. "Ruang pai thieo hua muang lao fai tawan ook" [Visiting the eastern Lao towns], *Wachirayan* 5 (1896), 25–30.

12. Interview S:116.

13. Interview C:22.

14. Interview S:116.

15. See fn. 14

16. Interview I:169.

17. Interview I:132, I:165.

18. Interview S:97.

19. Interview S:121, S:81.

20. Interview C:42.

21. National Archives SP. 2.8/6 Memoir compiled by Prince Damrong on dam irrigation 1923

22. National Archives R.5 M.46/4 16 October ro. so. 111 (1892).

23. Bunchuai Srisawat, *Thai sipsongpanna*, 590.

24. Royal Irrigation Department, "The Greater Chao Phraya Project," February 1967, cited in Suntharee Asawai, "Kan phatthana," 13. The worst famine year was 1919 when the rains failed, see Suntharee Asawai and Niti Kasikoson, "Wikritkan thang sethakit lang songkhram lok krang thi 1" [Economic crisis after the First World War] (Bangkok: Thai Khadi Suksa, 1982).

25. Interview C:32.

26. Dilok, *Landwirtschaft*, chapter 3.

27. See the later drop in statistics of production per rai over 1907–1960, *Sathiti kan kaset khong prathet thai 2509* [Agricultural Statistics of Thailand 1966] (Bangkok: Agricultural Economics Department, 1968), 46–7.

28. Interview C:3.

29. Interview C:22.

30. Interview I:127.

31. Interview C:25

32. Interview Sengiam Ditcharoen (not in interview list).

33. Interview S:96.

34. K. S. R. Kulap, "Rabiap kan tam na" [Rice farming], *Sayam prathet*, V, 45, 27 February ro. so. 123 (1904), 1172–80.

35. See Sukhothai Inscription No. 1, "In the water there are fish, in the field there is rice" *Prachum silacharuk* [Collected inscriptions] (Bangkok: Prime Minister's Office 1963). Nicolas Gervaise stated that the main food of the Siamese was rice, fish, and vegetables, see Gervaise, *Natural and Political History*, 73–5; Bishop Pallegoix wrote: "La nourriture ordinaire des Thais consiste en riz, poissons, légumes et fruits" [the ordinary food of the Thais consists of rice, fish, vegetables, and fruit], *Description*, 62; Satow, a British consular official in Siam, stated similarly that apart from rice the main food was fish, see FO. 69/90, "Mr Archer: Report on the country traversed by Mr Satow in his journey to Chiang Mai in December 1885, and January 1886," 3 April 1886, 6; Reverend N. A.

McDonald wrote that the main food of the Siamese was rice and fish, see *Siam: Its Government, Manners, Customs* (Philadelphia: Alfred Martien, 1871), 98.

36. Interview I:132.

37. Interview S:95, S:93.

38. Interview I:132.

39. Interview C:28

40. Interview I:132. Several old fishing tools can be seen at the cultural centre, Nakhon Sithammarat Teachers College.

41. Interview C:8.

42. Interview S:110.

43. See fn. 42

44. Interview C:25.

45. Interview S:117.

46. Interview C:1.

47. See fn. 46; Pallegoix, *Description*, 159; interview C:48.

48. Interview C:36.

49. Interview S:116.

50. Interview S:110.

51. Pallegoix, *Description*, 158–9; interviews C:41, C:24, I:127.

52. Interview I:168.

53. Interview I:148, S:117, C:24.

54. Interview I:148.

55. Achan Piyachat Pitawan interviewed villagers of Nawa Tai, king-amphoe Phosai, amphoe Khemmarat, Ubon Ratchathani, 14 March 1983.

56. Interviews C:18, N:73, C:51.

57. *Lokkathat thai phak tai* [World-view of southern region Thai] (Songkhla: Srinakharintharawirot University, Centre for Language and Culture of the Southern Region, 1978), 73.

58. Interview C:58.

59. Rev. John H. Freeman, *An Oriental Land of the Free or Life and Mission Work among the Laos of Siam, Burma, China and Indo-China* (Philadelphia: Westminster Press, 1910), 29; interviews C:15, C:42, I:168.

60. FO 69/90, "Report on the country traversed by Mr Satow," 7; interviews S:103, S:90, C:25, I:136, I:137, N:73, I:132, I:165, N:75, C:58.

61. *Prachum prakat ratchakan thi 4* [Collected proclamations of the Fourth Reign] vol 3, 1864, no. 253 (Bangkok: Khurusapha 1961), 232; Carl Bock recorded in 1881 that "These garments are generally home-spun, nearly every house having, either in one of the rooms or in the space under the house, a native loom," *Temples and Elephants* (London: Sampson Low, Marston, Searle & Rivington, 1884), 324.

62. Interview C:32.

63. Interview C:26.

64. Interview C:58, I:137, I:129, N:72.

65. Interview C:26.

66. Interview I:168; Pallegoix, *Description*; Khun Ratanavetchasaka, "Prapheni".

67. Pallegoix, *Description*, 59–60.

68. Interview C:6; Sangop Songmuang, "Chak sakdina su thun niyom: bot suksa kan plian plaeng prawatisat sethakit phak tai" [From sakdina to capitalism: study of historical change in the southern economy], typescript, Srinakharintharawirot University, Songkhla, 4 August 1983, chapter 3.

69. Sangop "Chak sakdina," chapter 3.

70. Interview C:1.

71. Interview Ma Kawinna (not in interview list), C:12.

72. Interview N:73, C:30.

73. Interview N:73; Khun Rattanawetchasakha "Prapheni"; the Lua are the same as the Kha. They call themselves Khamu, and are the same as Suai and the forest Khmer, calling themselves Kuai, and are old inhabitants of the territory now Thailand, see Jit Phumisak, *Kho thet ching waduai chonchat khom* [Facts about the Khom people] (Bangkok: Maingam), 91–5; James McCarthy (*Surveying and Exploring*, 92) wrote that the Khamu "are sturdy and hard-working foresters, content with very small remuneration. They are all spirit-worshippers."

74. See fn. 66

75. Data from a source who spent a long time with these people.

76. Sangop "Chak sakdina"; Bunrot Kaeokanha, "Kan kep suai nai samai rattanakosin ton ton" [Tax collection in the early Rattanakosin period], M.A. thesis, Chulalongkorn University, 1975; Suwit Thirasatsawat, "Prawatisat

sethakit kan muang thai tang tae samai somdet phrachao taksin maharat thung samai ratchakan thi 3 (pho. so. 2310–2394)" [History of the Thai political economy from Taksin to the Third Reign, 1767–1851], paper submitted to the National Research Council, 16 February 1982.

77. Crawfurd, *Journal*, 408–9; Wachirayan Archive, R.3 no. 111, 1908, official letters ordering Chachoengsao, Nakhon Nayok, and Prachinburi to accelerate delivery of tax to Bangkok for the second and third month to be in time for the monsoon bringing the junks, show clearly that this *suai* tax was collected for the purpose of state export.

78. Ammar Siamwalla, "Foreign Trade and Domestic Economy in Siam (1820–1855)," undated mimeo; rice exports valued 166,185 rupees out of total exports of 1,128,785 rupees.

79. D. E. Malloch, *Siam: Some General Remarks on its Productions* (Calcutta: Baptist Mission Press, 1852), 7; and see Ronald D. Renard, "Kariang: History of Karen-T'ai relations from the Beginnings to 1923," Ph.D. thesis, University of Hawaii, 1980, which states that the Karen supplied lac, tin, hides, and skins for export.

80. Ammar, "Foreign Trade," 4.6.

81. Ammar, "Foreign Trade," 4.6–4.7.

82. Crawfurd, *Journal*, 406–15.

83. Interviews C:30, C:24; Phra Maha Pricha Prinyano, *Prapheni boran thai isan* [Old Thai Isan customs] (Ubon Ratchathani: Siritham, 1952), 197–8; Lilian Johnson Curtis, *The Laos of North Siam* (1903), 59; Bunchuai Srisawat, *Lu: khon thai nai prathet chin thai sipsongpanna* [The Lue: Thai in China, the Sipsongpanna Thai] vol. 2 (Bangkok, 1955), 62.

84. Interviews I:172, I:136, I:165.

85. Sir John Bowring, *The Kingdom and People of Siam* (Kuala Lumpur, Oxford University Press, 1969), 81.

86. Dilok, *Landwirtschaft*.

87. Calculated from statistics in B. R. Mitchell, *International Historical Statistics, Africa and Asia* (New York and London: New York University Press, 1982), 43–5.

88. Dilok, *Landwirtschaft*; Matsen Rattanatrang (S:116) of amphoe Sikao, Trang, said in interview that twenty families was called a village, and Tit Tankai

(N:71) of amphoe Thungchang, Nan, said two or three houses was already a village for him.

89. National Archives R.5 M.46/6, household registration 25 December ro. so. 115 (1896).

90. Interview C:58.

91. Interview I:127.

92. Interview S:90.

93. Charuwan, "Sethasat".

94. Interviews I:137, N:64; Sanphachai Yancharoen "Dong Noi" (Dong Noi village, tambon Kokko, amphoe Muang, Lopburi), student research paper for history course 211 of Achan Charuk Bunchai, Thepsatri Teachers College, 1980; Charles F. Keyes, "In Search of Land: Village Formation in the Central Chi River Valley, Northeastern Thailand," *Contributions to Asian Studies* IX, 45–63.

95. The Mon came in 1600, 1660, 1774, and 1814, see Ministry of Commerce and Communications, *Siam, Nature and Industry* (Bangkok, 1930), 94; Thoetsak Maharuansong, "Ruan mon thi lopburi" [Mon abode in Lopburi], thesis for advanced certificate, faculty of architecture, graduate school, Silpakorn University, 1977, 21–3. Among villagers on the left bank of the Mekong who were rounded up and moved in after the suppression of the Chao Anu revolt, especially in 1828, 1830, 1836 and 1841, the Phuan migrated in 1834 from their old location in Xieng Khouang to the southeast of Luang Prabang, see Chatchawan Sukhanthawiphat, *Prawat khwam pen ma khong tai phuan* [History of the Thai Phuan], cremation volume of Captain Sanit Sukhanthawiphat (Bangkok: Witayakan, 1980); the Lao Song or Lao Songdam or Black Thai used to live in Sipsong Chuthai, later moved to Xieng Khouang, Vientiane, Khammuan, Savannakhet, Saravane, and into Thailand during the Fifth Reign and before, see Kusuma Chaiwinit and Charuwan Thammawat, "Prapheni chapho klum tai dam" [Customs of the Black Thai], *Isan Parithat* [Isan review] (Bangkok: Krungsayam, 1980); Phu Thai who used to live in Na Noi Ooi Nu on the Lao side, were rounded up and moved to Siam after the war with Chao Anu in 1828, see Phra Photiwongsachan Tisso Uan "Prawat chon chat phu thai" [History of the Phu Thai], *Latthi thamniam tang tang* [Various traditions] I, 1 (Bangkok: Khlangwithaya, 1972), Thawin Kesonrat,

*Prawat phu thai* [History of the Phu Thai] (Bangkok: Krungsayam, 1969), *Prachum phongsawadan* [Collected Chronicles] 4, 33, Third Reign Chronicle of Chaophraya Thiphakorawong. The population of Saiburi was rounded up by Chaophraya Nakhon (Noi) and brought to Bangkok and Nakhon Sithammarat in 1822, see Prince Damrong, *Phraratcha-phongsawadan krung rattanakosin* [Bangkok chronicles], Second Reign, vol. 2 (Phranakhon: Khurusapha, 1971), 116–7; interviews S:119, S:108, Ms Chinda Panphong (not in interview list).

    96. Interviews C:14, C:1, C:30, C:51, Plian Iammaroeng, N:72, S:87, Da Wongkham.

    97. Interview S:93.

    98. Interviews S:103, S:106.

    99. Interview I:163

    100. Interviews C:41, C:25; Achan Piyachat Pitawan interviewed villagers in Nawa Tai, tambon Samrong, king-amphoe Khemmarat, Ubon Ratchathani, 15 March 1983.

    101. Interview I:132.

    102. Interviews I:137, I:156, I:169.

    103. Interviews S:117, I:148, S:90, C:25, I:165, C:6.

    104. See fn. 96.

    105. See the original, "Kap pu son lan" [Ballad of the grandfather teaching his grandchildren], in Sittha Phinitphuwadon, *Naeo tang sangkhep khong wicha wannakhadi priap thiap* [Short discourse on comparative literature] (Bangkok: Akson Charoentat 1980), 146–53.

    106. Interview I:165.

    107. Interview with villagers in Nawa Tai, tambon Samrong, king-amphoe Khemmarat, Ubon Ratchathani, 15 March 1983.

    108. Interview I:170; *Phun Khun Boromaratchathirat chabap sombun* [About Khun Boromaratchathirat, full version] Vientiane: Department of Lao Literature, 134, cited in Nikhom Charumani, "Prawatisat sangkhom hua muang samai ton krungthep: kan suksa korani phak tawan ok chiang nua" [Social history of major towns in the early Bangkok period: study of the northeast], roneo; Surasing Samruam Chimphanao, "Kho sangket bang prakan nai kan suksa watthanatham prapheni lanna choeng manutsawithaya" [Issues in the anthropological study of Lanna culture and traditions], conference papers on

*Phleng phun ban lanna thai* [Northern thai local music], volume 1/4, 21 January 1981; Andrew Turton, "Matrilineal Descent Groups and Spirit Cults of the Thai Yuan in Northern Thailand," *Journal of the Siam Society*, 20, 2 (1972); Turton found "a system of matrilineal descent groups and associated cults" (217) and noted "after the marriage ceremony the son-in-law fulfils his minimal obligation to provide raw meat, cook it and offer it to his wife's lineage spirit and lineage elder" (221).

109. Interview S:88.

110. Thomas E. Lux, "The Internal Structure and External Relations of a Northeastern Village," final research report submitted to the National Research Council of Thailand, Bangkok, December 1966, 24; Thawat Punnotok, *Wannakam isan* [Isan literature] (Bangkok: Odeon Store, 1980), 335; Thawat states that in the work "thammada son lok" [everyman teaches the world], the writer wishes to teach humans to have kinship ties. When I said goodbye at the close of the interview with Somsri Wongkraso, he replied "go wherever but always have brethren".

111. Takashi Tomosugi, "Landownership in Historical Perspective," in *A Structural Analysis of Thai Economic History* (Tokyo, Institute of Developing Economies, 1980), 104.

112. Interview C:6.

113. Interview C:51.

114. Interview I:135, S:82.

115. Pallegoix, *Description*, 76.

116. Katherine Bowie, "In the Wake of the Lords: A Historical Perspective on the Role of Irrigation in the Political Economy of Northern Thailand," mimeo, July 1980, 12.

117. Chai Ruangsin, *Prawatisat thai samai pho. so. 2352–2453 dan sethakit* [Thai economic history, 1809–1910] (Bangkok: Munnithi Khrongkan Tamra, 1979), 132; Pallegoix, *Description*, 119–20.

118. Interview I:182; Gutzlaff, *Journal of Two Voyages*, 31–2; Renard, "Kariang," 128–9; National Archives R.5 M.57/29 royal decree 18/8 year of the cock, seventh year of the decade, 1247; R.5 M.2.12 K-2 public notice to Nakhon Phanom 3 10 year of the cock 1247, Phra Phanom Natdanuraksitrat report to prime minister; R.5 M.2.12 K./19 public notice to various towns ro.

so. 104 (1884). Phraya Maha-ammattayathibodi report to the King; National Archives R.5 special volume 3, 5, 7 year of the rat, tenth year of decade, 1250, Phra Phirenthorathep, minister for police, to the honorary jury at the court.

119. Interviews N:72, S:118, C:29, C:44, S:107; Pallegoix, *Description*, 119–20.

120. Information from interviews in many villages in many localities.

121. Interview I:149.

122. Chatthip Nartsupha and Suthy Prasartset, "Rabop sethakit thai 1851–1910" [Thai economy 1851–1910] in Chatthip Nartsupha et al., *Sethasat kap prawatisat thai* [Thai economy and history] (Bangkok: Sangsan 1980), 144.

123. National Archives R.5 M.2.14/20 Prince Damrong to younger brother, Krommakhun Sommot Amoraphan, royal secretary, 11 May ro. so. 127 (1908).

124. Crawfurd, *Journal*, 374–5, 386.

125. Interview N:73.

126. Kennon Breazeale, "The Integration of the Lao States into the Thai kingdom," Ph.D. thesis, University of Oxford, 1975.

127. Announcement for the two princes to head the tattooing for corvée, 9 April ro. so. 74 (1855), *Prachum kotmai prachamsok* [Collected laws of the period], vol. 4/58, 96–9; National Archives R.4 kalahom (kh), vol 19, 165–73, Chaophraya Akkramahasena to governors of Nakhon Sithammarat, Songkhla, Phatthalung, Chumphon, Patiu, Kamnoet Nophakun, Chaiya, Langsuan, Phangnga, Takuapa, Takuathung, 27 July ro. so. 79 (1860).

128. Interview S:116.

129. Anchali Susayan, "Khwam plian plaeng khong rabop phrai lae phon kratop to sangkhom thai nai ratchasamai phrabatsomdet phrachulachomklao chaoyuhua" [Change in the *phrai* system and its impact on Thai society in the reign of King Chulalongkorn], M.A. thesis, Chulalongkorn University, 1981.

130. For example see Phornphen Hantrakun and Atcharaphon Kamutphitsamai (eds.), *Khwam chua phrasriariya* [Belief in the future Buddha] and *Khabot phumibun* [Holy men revolts] (Bangkok: Sangsan, 1984).

131. Chusit Chuchat, "Pho kha wua tang: phu bukboek kan kha khai nai muban phak nua khong prathet thai (pho. so. 2398–2503)" [Cattle traders: pioneers of trading in the villages of northern Thailand, 1855–1960], roneo, 1 August 1982; interviews N:67, N:73, N:78.

132. Interviews I:137, I:122.

133. Interview S:91, S:97.

134. Interview I:137; Chusit, "Pho kha wua tang".

135. Chusit, "Pho kha wua tang".

136. Interview I:147.

137. Interview C:28, C:51.

138. Interviews I:150, I:177, I:137; Jit, *Kho thet ching*, 17–9; *Phochananukrom chabap ratchabanthitsathan pho. so. 2525* [Royal Institute Dictionary 1982] (Bangkok: Aksoncharoentat, 1982), 105, 323. Acording to the dictionary, the Kula by race are Tongsu and Thai Yai. Tongsu are a group of Karen or Yang.

139. Interviews N:67, S:119, S:97.

140. Interview I:127; Pranut Sapphayasan, "Wiwatthanakan sethakit muban nai phak tawan ook chiang nua khong prathet pho. so. 2394–2475" [Development of the village economy in the northeast, 1851–1932], M.A. thesis, Chulalongkorn University, 1982; "Ruang pai thieo hua muang lao fai tawan ook" [Visiting the main towns of eastern Lao], *Wachirayan* 5 (1896), 25.

141. Interviews I:182, I:179, N:72, I:149, I:128.

142. Interview C:51.

143. Interviews S:90, S:100; Sangop Songmuang, "Chak sakdina," chapter 3.

144. Interview I:132.

145. Wirawat Pinkhian, "Wannakam krariang chak tambon suan phung king amphoe suan phung changwat ratchaburi" [Karen literature from Suan Phung, Ratchaburi], department of Thai language, Chombung Teachers College, 1982, "Ruang khon bon khao" [About hill people]; National Archives R.6 M.65.2/1 Phraya Sisahathep, permanent secretary, report to Krommakhun Sommot Amoraphan, royal secretary, 14 January ro. so. 139 (1920); Sarawuth Thiwan "Raingan prawatisat muban" [Report on village history], submitted to Achan Yupin Khemmuk, Chiang Mai Teachers College, 1982.

146. Interviews S:103, S:106, S:90, S:116; the northern boat lapsed only in 1967 when the road was completed to the edge of the hills and then only road transport was used.

147. Interview S:111.

148. Interview I:144; Charubut Ruangsawan, "Sieo" [Friendship], *Watthanatham thai* [Thai culture], 20, 1 (January 1981).

149. Interview Achan Chatchai Sukrakan, department of anthropology and social science, Nakhon Sithammarat Teachers College, 24–5 January 1981.

150. Interview I:144; Sarawut, "Raingan"; National Archives R.6 M.14.2/1 Phraya Sisahathep, permanent secretary, report to Krommakhun Sommot Amoraphan, royal secretary, 14 January ro. so. 129 (1910).

151. McCarthy, *Surveying and Exploring*, 114–5; Interview N:78, S:90, S:100.

152. Interview Achan Suwat Nuphinit, Sapha Ratchini school, Trang, 2 May 1983.

153. Bunchuai Srisawat, *Thai sipsongpanna*, 197; Interview N:69.

154. Nithi Eosiwong, *Watthanatham kradumphi kap wannakam ton rattanakosin* [Bourgeois culture and early Rattanakosin literature] (Bangkok: Thai Khadi Studies Institute, 1982), chapter 3; Sirilak Sakkriangkrai, *Ton kamnoet khong chonchan nai thun nai prathet thai (pho. so. 2398–2453)* [Rise of capitalist class in Thailand, 1855–1910] (Bangkok: Sangsan, 1981); Yada Praphaphan, *Rabop chao phasi nai akorn samai krungthep yuk ton* [Tax-farming system in the early Bangkok period] (Bangkok: Sangsan, 1981), chapters 3 and 4.

155. Nithi, *Watthanatham kradumphi*.

156. Sirilak, *Ton kamnoet*, 41–2; G. William Skinner, *Chinese Society in Thailand: An Analytical History* (New York: Cornell University Press, 1975), 74, 75, 78, 80.

157. "Kan pokkhrong khong khon chat lao tawan ok" [Administration of the eastern Lao], *Wachirayan* 5 (1896), 2494–5; National Archives R.5 M.57/29 royal command 188 year of the cock, seventh year of the decade, 1247, given to Chao Yutitham, ruler of Champassak; National Archives SP. 2.56/68, names of towns founded in Rattanakosin.

158. Luang Padung Kwaenprachan Chan-uttaranakhon "Latthi thamniam ratsadon phak isan" [Customs of Isan people], *Latthi thamniam tang tang* [Various customs] part 1 (Bangkok: Khlangwithaya, 1972).

159. Interview C:51; Norake Photibetwongsa, "Tamnan thaiphu-thaiwang" [Traditions of Buddhist Thai-palace Thai] typescript, Kalasin, 1976, 103.

160. Nophachon Itthichicharat "Khwam chua nai phisang wetmon khong chaona thai nai phak nua" [The northern villagers' belief in spirit worship and

magic], *Phuthasasana nai lanna thai* [Buddhism in northern Thailand] (Chiang Mai: Thipyanet, 1980); *Lokkathat thai phak tai*, 126–7.

161.Interview I:165.

162.Nophachon, "Khwam chua"; interview with Achan Surasing Samruam Chimphanao, Chiang Rai Teachers College, 28 December 1981.

163.Suthep Sunthornphesat "Khwam chua ruang 'phi puya' nai muban tawan ook chiang nua" [Belief in ancestor spirits in northeastern villages] in Suthep (ed.), *Sangkhomwithaya khong muban phak tawan ook chiang nua* [Sociology of northeastern villages] (Bangkok: Social Science Association of Thailand, 1968); interview I:148; Fong Sitthitham, "Silpa-watthanatham," 147.

164.Interview N:69.

165.Tanabe, "Guardian Spirit Cults"; Sanguan Chotisukharat, *Prapheni thai phak nua* [Northern thai customs] (Bangkok: Sanguan, 1966), 20; "Kan pokkhrong," 2509; Bunchuai, *Thai sipsongpanna*, 235, 367–8, 595–7.

166."Kan napthu chao lae phi" [Belief in spirits], *Wachirayan* 5 (1896), 25–30.

167.Arunrat, "Kan wikhro sangkhom chiangmai"; *Tamnan phun muang chiangmai*, 11.

168.*Lokkathat thai phak tai*, 126–8; interview S:94.

169.On the Thachin river between Bangso and Bangsam, amphoe Songphinong, Suphanburi.

170.Interview I:151; Sumit Pitiphan "Khon thai nai sipsongpanna" [The Thai in Sipsongpanna], *Warasan thammasat*, 12, 1 (March 1983), 136. Sumit states that the Thai of Tongkin or Black Tai still retain these old beliefs; interview I:141.

171.Suwit Sangyokha, "Prapheni bang yang nai phak klang: prapheni thi nuang duai achip tam na tham rai" [Some customs of the central region: customs connected with farming], *Sombat thai* [Thai treasures] (Lopburi: Thepsatri Teachers College, 1981), 73–84; interviews S:106, Rik Aebu (not in interview list), I:132, S:97, S:99; Sukhothai Inscription 1.

172.Presbyterian Board of Publications, *Siam and Laos* (Philadelphia, 1884), 242, 509; McDonald, *Siam*; Freeman, *Oriental Land*, 43, 45; C. H. Dessman, "Lights and Shadows of the Days," *The Laos News* 3, 1 (January 1905), 27–8; Daniel McGilvary, *A Half Century among the Siamese and the Lao: An*

*Autobiography* (New York: Fleming H. Revelco, 1912), 204, 266; Arunrat, "Kan wikhro sangkhom chiangmai," 266; Charuwan Thammawat *Khati chaoban isan* [Sayings of Isan villagers] (Bangkok: Aksonwatthana, n.d.), 1–9; J. W. McKean, "Extension of Medical Work in Chiang Mai," *The Laos News* 4, 4 (October 1907); interview C:38.

173. Curtis, *The Laos*, 225–6.

174. Pallegoix, *Description*, 18–9; Curtis, *The Laos*, 225; McCarthy, *Surveying and Exploring*, 92, 131; Thawat Bunnotok, "Khwam chua phun ban an samphan kap withi chiwit nai sangkhom isan" [Local beliefs connected with way-of-life in Isan society], paper for seminar on local culture, beliefs, arts and language, Bangkok 8–10 September 1983; James C. Scott, "Protest and Profanation: Agrarian Revolts and the Little Tradition," *Theory and Society*, 2, 4 (1977).

175. Interview C:51.

176. Interview I:165.

177. Gervaise, *Natural and Political History*, 43; National Archives R.5 M.2 14/22, report of Phaya Sarit on the inspection of monthon Nakhon Sithammarat, ro. so. 113 (1894); interviews C:51, C:24.

178. Interview I:165; Chaophraya Surasakmontri (Choem Saeng-Xuto), *Latthi thamniam tang tang* [Various customs] part 5, about forest peoples of various nationalities.

179. Kanoksak Kaewthep, "Raingan phon kan wichai ruang prawat kan khluanwai khong chaona thai chak adit-patchuban: botwikhro thang sethasat kanmuang" [Research report on Thai village movements from the past to the present: a political economy analysis], presented to the Social Science Association of Thailand, 1 June 1983.

180. See fn. 174

181. Freeman, *Oriental Land*, 45.

182. See fns. 174 and 181; Charuwan, "Khati chaoban," 1–13; Chatthip and Pranut, "Udomkan".

183. Even today, Buddhism is not established among the So of amphoe Kusuman, Sakon Nakhon, the Kha of king amphoe Dong Luang, Nakhon Phanom, and the Suai of amphoe Khunhan, Sisaket, for example.

184. Chatthip and Pranut, "Udomkan".

# CHAPTER THREE

1. In 1900, exports from Indonesia in rank order were sugar, coffee, tobacco; from Malaya, tin, rubber; from Philippines, jute, sugar, dried coconut; see Mitchell, *International Historical Statistics*, 486–7.

2. Ingram, *Economic Change*, 44.

3. Chatthip Nartsupha, "Foreign Trade, Foreign Finance and the Economic Development of Thailand, 1959–1965," Ph.D. thesis, Tufts University, 1968, 23.

4. Suwit Paithayawat, *Wiwatthanakan sethakit chonnabot nai phak klang khong prathet thai rawang pho. so. 2394–2475* [Rural economic development in the central region 1851–1932] (Bangkok: Sangsan, 1978), tables on pages 163–7, using data from British Consular Report, Comparative Statistics of Imports and Exports of the Kingdom of Siam.

5. Ingram, *Economic Change*, 94

6. Ingram, *Economic Change*, 37–41, 52–4.

7. Dilok, *Landwirtschaft*, chapter 3.

8. J. Homan van der Heide, "The Economical Development of Siam during the Last Half-Century," *Journal of the Siam Society*, 3 (1906), 77–80.

9. National Archives R.5 KS.1/11, Director General, Royal Irrigation Department to Minister of Agriculture, 20 May 1907.

10. Ingram, *Economic Change*, 44

11. Carle C. Zimmerman, *Siam: Rural Economic Survey, 1930–31* (Bangkok: Bangkok Times, 1931), 174.

12. Zimmerman, *Siam*, 173.

13. Zimmerman, *Siam*, 199.

14. Zimmerman, *Siam*, 129.

15. Ingram, *Economic Change*, 53

16. Zimmerman, *Siam*, 19.

17. "Kam hai kan khun luang wat pradu songtham" [Evidence given by Khun Luang Wat Pradu Songtham], *Thalaengkan prawatisat ekasan borankhadi* [Historical bulletin of archaeological documents], 3, 1, January 1972; Chai Ruangsin, *Prawatisat thai samai pho. so. 2357–2453 dan sethakit* [Thai economic history 1814–1910] (Bangkok: Mulniti Krongkan Damra, 1979).

18. Pallegoix, *Description*, 3.

19. Shigeharu Tanabe, "Land Reclamation in the Chao Phraya Delta," in *Thailand*, ed. Ishii, 40–82; David B. Johnston, "Opening a Frontier: The Expansion of Rice Cultivation in Central Thailand in the 1890s," *Contributions to Asian Studies*, IX, 27–44.

20. J. Homan van der Heide, *General Report on Irrigation and Drainage in the Lower Menam Valley*, Bangkok, 1930, 26 fn., 66; Sunthari, *Prawat khrongkan rangsit*, 158–9, citing National Archives KS. 3.2/28 vol 2.

21. Interview C:36.

22. Kitti Tanthai, "Khlong kap rabop sethakit thai (pho. so. 2367–2453)" [Canals and the Thai economic system, 1824–1910], M.A. thesis, Chulalongkorn University, 1977, 119.

23. Sunthari Asawai, "Kan phatthana rabop cholaprathan nai prathet thai tangtae pho. so. 2431 thung pho. so. 2491" [Development of irrigation systems in Thailand from 1888 to 1948], *Aksonsat niphon* [Arts bulletin] 1, eds. Wilatwong Phongsabut, Busakon Kanchanachari, Suwadi Thonprasitphatthana (Bangkok: Thepprathan, 1982), 58; Sunthari, *Prawat khrongkan rangsit*, chapter 4.

24. Ammar Siamwalla, "Land, Labour and Capital in Three Rice-Growing Deltas of Southeast Asia, 1800–1940," discussion paper 150, Yale University, 1972.

25. Interviews C:42, C:30, C:47, C:52.

26. Wachirayan Archive R.4 J.S. 1222 no. 117, royal command on law about grant of house, land, paddy field, orchard, 7 April ro. so. 80 (1861).

27. Interview C:30.

28. Interviews C:1, C:3, C:53.

29. Interviews C:1, C:11, C:28, C:52, C:24, C:6.

30. Interview C:26.

31. Interview C:15.

32. Interview C:52.

33. Interview C:39.

34. Interview C:38.

35. Interview C:27.

36. Interviews C:11, C:44; Yada, "Rabop chao phasi".

37. Interviews C:36, C:53

38. Interview C:48.

39. Interview C:32.

40. Skinner, *Chinese Society*, 105.

41. Interview C:32.

42. Interviews C:28, C:52.

43. Interview C:44.

44. Interview C:51.

45. Interviews C:28, C:52, C:39.

46. Interview C:18

47. National Archives R.7 KS. 15.2/22, Siam's imports.

48. Interview C:32.

49. Skinner, *Chinese Society*, 214.

50. Interviews C:15, C:51.

51. Interviews C:50, C:48, C:61.

52. Interviews C:1, C:39, C:51.

53. Interviews C:27, C:22.

54. Interview C:27.

55. Phraya Suriyanuwat, *Sapphasat* [Economics] (Bangkok: Phikanet, third ed.,1975), 71–2.

56. National Archives R.6 KS. 3.1/11, memorandum on measures to counter the recession and restore prosperity, 29 October ro. so. 129 (1910).

57. Phra aiyakan laksana ku ni matra 50 [Law on debt clause 50] *Kotmai tra sam duang*, vol. 1 (Bangkok: Khurusapha, 1963).

58. Dilok, *Landwirtschaft*; Zimmerman, *Siam*, 317–8, 195.

59. Zimmerman, *Siam*, 204–5.

60. Interviews C:1, C:58, C:8.

61. Interview C:58.

62. National Archives R.6 N.19/32, Phraya Suntharaburi, provincial commissioner, inspector of monthon Nakhon Chaisi, to Chaophraya Yommarat, minister of interior, 30 December 1923; National Archives R.7 P.13/5, economic depression impact on farmers in Ang Thong; *Prasopakan lae khwam hen bang prakan khong ratthaburut awuso pridi phanomyong* [Experience and some views of elder statesman, Pridi Banomyong] (Bangkok: Project on Pridi Banomyong and Thai society, 1983), 37.

63. National Archives R.7 RS.19.3/37, "Siam's Young King Foils Unique Plot," *New York Times*, 30 March 1932; interview C:51.

64. Interviews C:39, C:8, C:1.

65. Interview C:23.

66. Interviews C:32, C:8.

67. Chatthip, "Foreign Trade," 27 fn. 9.

68. Interviews C:58, C:10, C:28; National Archives R.6 N.43/3, Ratburana district officer to Khun Phra Phetprani, head of district office, 18 September ro. so. 130 (1911).

69. Interview C:31; Thawisin Supwatthana, "Kan khloen yai raengngan isan khao su suan klang nai adit" [Movement of Isan labour into the central region in the past], paper for Thai studies conference, 10–11 January 1983, Srinakharinthara-wirot University, Mahasarakham; National Archives R.5 R.3.2 K/63 Phraya Ratsadakoson to Krommaluang Naret Worarit, 6 February ro. so. 125 (1906).

70. Zimmerman, *Siam*, 18.

71. Interview C:58.

72. Interview C:58.

73. Akin Rabibhadana, *The Organisation of Thai Society in the Early Bangkok Period, 1782–1873* (New York: Cornell data paper 74, 1969), 178.

74. Interviews C:27, C:51, S:90.

75. Interview C:58.

76. Interview C:51.

77. Interview C:1

78. Interview C:1.

79. Interview C:27.

## CHAPTER FOUR

1. Anan Kanchaphan (Ganjanapan), "The Partial Commercialization of Rice Production in Northern Thailand (1900–1981)," Ph.D. thesis, Cornell University, 1984, 101–2.

2. Anan, "Partial Commercialization," 111–4.

3. Anan, "Partial Commercialization," 103, table 3.1, adapted from Suthy Pra-sartset, "A Study of Production and Trade in Thailand," Ph.D. thesis, Sydney University, 1975, 264; British Consular Reports 1898, 1904.

4. Chusit, "Pho kha wua tang".

5. Interview C:3.

6. Chatthip Nartsupha and Suthy Prasartset, "Rabop sethakit thai 1851–1910" [Thai economic system 1851–1910] (Bangkok: Sangsan, 1981), 131.

7. Interview N:65

8. Anan, "Partial Commercialization," 85, 90.

9. Anan, "Partial Commercialization," 79–146.

10. Anan, "Partial Commercialization," 94; Chusit Chuchat, "Khabot phayaphap (prab songkhram) khabot chaona nai phak nua" [The Phayaphap revolt: a farmers revolt in the north], *Warasan sangkhomsat* [Social science journal] Chiang Mai University, 3, 2 (October 1979–March 1980); Saratsawadi Ongsakun, "Khabot phrayaphrap songkhram mae tap muang chiangmai pho. so. 2432" [Revolt of Phraya Phrap Songkhram, army chief of Chiang Mai 1889], roneo 1982; Tej Bunnag; "Khabot ngieo muang phrae ro. so. 121" [Ngieo revolt in Phrae 1902], *Sangkhomsat parithat* [Social science review] 6, 2 (September–November 1978).

11. Interview N:65; FO 371/9251, British Embassy to Marquess Curzon, 27 December 1922; Chusit, "Wiwatthanakan," 65.

12. Anan, "Partial Commercialization," 148; Ingram, *Economic Change*, 47.

13. Ingram, *Economic Change*, 47.

14. Anan, "Partial Commercialization," 116–21; National Archives R.6 M.30, Monthon Phayap; interview N:77.

15. Anan, "Partial Commercialization," 169–80.

16. Anan, "Partial Commercialization," 155.

17. Zimmerman, *Siam*, 18.

18. Chusit Chuchat, "Kan kamnoet rabop sethakit thun niyom kap phon krathop thi mi to sangkhom chaona nai phak nua pho. so. 2398–2475" [The rise of the capitalist system and its impact on farmers in the northern region 1855–1932], *Sangkhomsat* [Social science] 5, 1 (April–September 1981); Prani Sirithon na Phatthalung, *Phu bukboek haeng chiangmai* [Chiangmai pioneers] (Bangkok: Ruangsin, 1980); interview N:62.

19. Chusit, "Kan kamnoet".

20. Zimmerman, *Siam*, 170.

21. Chusit, "Kan kamnoet".

22. Interviews N:72, N:73.

23. Interview N:78.

24. Interview N:74.

25. Interviews of villagers in amphoe Sansai, Chiang Mai.

26. Phanni Uansakun, "Kitchakan muang rae dibuk kap kan plian plaeng thang sethakit phak tai prathet thai pho. so. 2411–2474" [Tin mining and economic change in southern Thailand 1868–1931], M.A. thesis, Chulalongkorn University, 1979, chapter 2; Phanni Uansakun, "Sethakit kan phanit tang prathet khong muang nakhon sithammarat rawang phutthasatawat thi 19–24" [Overseas commerce of Nakhon Sithammarat in the nineteenth to twenty-fourth centuries of the Buddhist era], *Raingan kan sammana prawatisat nakhon sithammarat* [Report of the conference on history of Nakhon Sithammarat] (Nakhon Sithammarat Teachers College and the National Cultural Commission, 1983), 275–91.

27. Phanni, "Sethakit".

28. Phanni, "Sethakit".

29. Phanni, "Sethakit"; Ingram, *Economic Change*, 240–2.

30. Phanni, "Kitchakan muang rae," chapter 4.

31. Phanni, "Kitchakan muang rae," chapter 4.

32. Second royal letter from the royal ship called Ubon Burathit parked at the mouth of Songkhla, 29 July ro. so. 108 (1889), to others and Krommaluang Thewawong Waropakan, royal secretary to King Chulalongkorn about visit to the Malay peninsula, ro. so. 108, 109, 117, 120 (1889, 1890, 1898, 1901), in total four times, printed for distribution at the cremation of his sister, Princess Malini Nopadara Siriniphaphannawadi Krommakhun Si Satchanalai Sukanya at Sanam Luang (Thai Printers, Rong Muang Rd, 1925).

33. Dilok, *Landwirtschaft*, chapter 3.

34. Interview S:103.

35. Ministry of Commerce and Communications, *Siam*, 275; interview S:112.

36. Sirin Bunsotharasathit, "Prawatisat sethakit chonnabot phak tai fang tawan ook phai lang sonthisanya baoring pho. so. 2398" [Rural economic history of the east of the southern region after the Bowring treaty 1855], report of first conference on history and society of Nakhon Sithammarat.

37. Interviews S:94, S:82.

38. Interview in 1983 with relatives of Phaya Phuminatphakdi (who died 47 years earlier) at his house in amphoe Muang, Satun.

39. Interviews S:87, S:92.

40. Zimmerman, *Siam*, 18.

41. Interview S:109.

42. Ingram, *Economic Change*, 94.

43. Rubber Research Centre Had Yai, *Kan songsoem lae kan phatthana yang* [Support and development of rubber], roneo (March 1982), 1, cited in Sangop, "Chak sakdina".

44. Interview S:97.

45. Interview Lik Aebu (not in interview list).

46. See fn. 45.

47. Zimmerman, *Siam*, 19.

48. Interview S:117.

49. Interview S:89.

50. Interview S:97.

51. Interviews S:87, S:92.

52. See fn. 51.

53. Interview with villagers of Nawa Tai, king-amphoe Phosai, amphoe Khemmarat, Ubon Ratchathani, 15 March 1983.

54. Interviews I:178, I:147

55. Interview I:139; Pranut, "Wiwatthanakan," 101; National Archives R.6 K 17/15 poll tax in monthon Ubon, 20 September 1914.

56. Ingram, *Economic Change*, 47.

57. See fn. 54; interviews I:126, I:167, I:181.

58. Interview I:178; Ministry of Commerce and Communications, *Economic Conditions*, 12.

59. Ministry of Commerce and Communications, *Economic Conditions*, 12.

60. National Archives R.6 N. 19/35.

61. Pranut, "Wiwatthanakan," 7; National Archives SP. 2.47/84, inspection report of provinces of Lomsak, Loei, Phetchabun in monthon Udon, April 1927, compiled by Nakhon Sawan Woraphinit, supreme councillor and minister of war (kalahom), 16 September 2430 (1887).

62. Ingram, *Economic Change*, 37; Suwit, *Wiwatthankan*, 163–8.

63. Pranut, "Wiwatthanakan".

64. *Somdet phrachaoboromwongtoe kromphraya damrong rachanuphap ruang thieo thi tang tang: phak thi 4 waduai tieo monthon ratchasima monthon udon lae monthon roi-et* [Travels of Prince Damrong, part 4, visits to monthons Ratchasima, Udon and Roi-et] (Bangkok: second edition, 1923), 12–3; Prince Damrong, *Nithan borankhadi* [Some ancient tales], printed in commemoration of the royal cremation of Rong Ammatekthasong Suwannasi at Wat That Thong, 25 April 1966.

65. James C. Scott, "Hegemony and the Peasantry," in *Southeast Asia in a Changing World*, ed. Shigekazu Matsumoto, proceedings and papers of a symposium held at the Institute of Developing Economies, 15–17 March 1978 (Tokyo: IDE, 1978), 193.

66. Chatthip and Pranut, "Udomkan".

67. Chusit, "Khabot"; Sarasawat, "Khabot".

68. Tej, "Khabot".

69. Tej Bunnag, "Phraya khaek jet hua muang kopkit khabot ro. so. 121" [Revolt of the seven provinces] in *Prawatisat lae watthanatham* [History and culture], 15–29, printed in honour of Krommamuan Narathip Phongpraphan on the occasion of eightieth birthday, 25 August 1971, (Bangkok: Social Science Association of Thailand, 1971); Somchot Ongsakkun, "Kan pathirup kan pokkhrong monthon pattani (pho. so. 2449–2474)" [Administrative reform in monthon Pattani, 1906–1931], M.A. thesis, Srinakharintharawirot University, 1978, 145–90.

70. Somchot Ongsakhun, "Khabot phu wiset: phi bun nai phak tai" [Holy men revolts in the south], *Warasan prawatisat* [Journal of history] 7, 1 (January 1982).

71. Chatthip and Pranut, "Udomkan".

72. Phra Achan Suwat Suwatcho "Achan mahathera prawat phra achan fan acharo" [Life of Achan Fan Acharo], *Khonphonlok* 9, 93 (April 1983), 92; the

incident took place at Ban Fu village, tambon Nonthan, amphoe Muang, Khon Kaen.

73. Interview I:145.
74. Interview I:151.
75. Interview I:172.
76. Interview I:136.
77. Interview I:172.
78. Data from a source who spent a long time with these people.
79. Interview C:16.
80. Interview C:50.

# APPENDIX 1

## QUESTION GUIDE FOR INTERVIEWING VILLAGERS

These questions were just a guide. During the actual interviews, the questions changed according to the background and experience of the interviewee. The actual interviews had an informal nature, more like a conversation, with questions simplified to help the interviewee understand because there were a lot of problems of culture and language. Even though many questions do not seem to specify a period, actual questioning always emphasised whether the question referred to the time the interviewee was a child, youth, or whether the interviewee was recalling what parents had said.

## Part 1. Questions about the interviewee

1. Name
2. Age and year of birth
3. Address (house number, hamlet, tambon, amphoe, province)
4. Tell the history of great-grandparents, grandparents, parents, all siblings, and self.

## Part 2. Questions about productive capacity

5.  Explain what kind of paddy you cultivate and why.
6.  Describe method of farming, especially technology used and objective in using, from the past to the present; did the method change and why.
7.  Any production or crop other than rice? Do any weaving? Describe the method of weaving, and the process of change in each period; if make anything else such as bamboo-weaving, carts, salt, collect forest goods, etc., explain in detail where the raw materials came from, and how made.
8.  Describe problems over water, local irrigation systems (*muang-fai*), digging ponds and canals.
9.  Is there any village which does only artisan work? Why or why not?
10. Why has weaving declined? Describe decline of local artisan work in detail.
11. Why no thought of expanding weaving or other artisan work in the village in the past, or producing for sale?
12. Describe the size of the surplus and what happens to it.

## Part 3. Questions about the foundation of the village and its population

13. When was this village founded? Why was it founded here?
14. How did the population size of the village change?
15. Describe causes of death, including deaths of children below one year, epidemics.
16. Describe customs of weddings, and family size.
17. Any migration or splitting off to found a village? How often? For what reasons? Explain the process.

## Part 4. Questions about bonds in production and the village community

18. Describe nature of land occupancy in the village, how land was acquired, and changes in the structure of land occupancy.
19. Describe particularly who are the large landholders and how they acquired land.
20. What is the rental rate? How has it changed since the past?
21. Where does the capital for farming or artisan production come from? If not own capital, borrowed from who? What interest?
22. Any common land in the village? Anything held in common?
23. Any cooperation in production between households in the village, or between villages? Any pooling of land or capital in production such as buffaloes or implements? Describe cooperation in labour.
24. Describe class structure and property system in the village.
25. Describe division of produce, within the family and within the village.
26. Describe local traders in the village, their rise, relations with ordinary villagers, type of goods they buy and sell; describe *nai hoi*, what do such people do with any surplus they have? Do they move out of the village to practise their trade in the town or not?
27. Describe the status, duties, and roles of women and children.

## Part 5. Questions about the superstructure of the village

28. Who administers within the village? Where does the administrative power come from? What economic status?
29. Describe the process of decision-making on matters which affect the whole village
30. Describe power and decision-making within the family, especially over production.

31. Describe the belief system of the village, rise and development of belief in spirits and Buddhism

32. Describe the influence of these beliefs on property rights and production, including the development of productive power.

33. Describe the rise and role of the *wat* in the village. What extent of land does the *wat* own? What surplus does the *wat* have from production?

34. Describe kin relations in the village, and any development in their nature. What effect do they have on property rights or the development of productive power in the village?

35. Is there really a soul? Rebirth? Do deeds in this life (*kamma*) affect any future life?

36. Any spirit shrine in the village? When was it founded? When the spirit enters the medium, what does it say? In nearby villages are there any?

37. When was the *wat* in the village founded? Why was it built? What do the monks teach? Why do you make merit? How often do you go to the *wat* to hear a sermon? Is today any different from the time of your parents or grandparents?

38. Have you heard of the future Buddha (*phra sriariya*)? When do you think he will come? What did your father and grandfather believe?

39. Why are certain people lords and masters? And some *phrai*? Who orders it? If you could return as a master, would you? And what would you do in the village?

40. Have you ever heard your great-grandparents, grandparents or parents talk or complain about any difficulties? What did they say were the causes of these difficulties? How did they want the village to be to make them most satisfied? What sort of ideal perfect society did they themselves want?

41. In the thinking of elders, what is a village? Who are capitalists? Who are nobles? Who are labourers? Who are monks? What is Thailand? (Ask the interviewee to reply in the words of elders.)

42. Why does it rain, storm, flood? What is the origin of hills, rivers and streams, various animals? How did man come into being? How do elders describe these things?
43. Why does the country change and prosper? Who makes it prosper? Is this prosperity a good thing? Or do you think not?
44. What is history?

## Part 6. Questions about the relations between the village and the outside world

45. Do you sell what you produce? For what reason? When did you start to sell? About what percentage of your total production?
46. Who comes to buy? Do you take it to sell yourself or does a middleman come in to buy? Why is it like this?
47. Do you sell any artisan products in the market? For what reason?
48. What relations are there between village and village? Especially economic relations?
49. Is the village self-sufficient or not? What goods do you need from the outside world? How do you get those goods?
50. Describe nature of communications with the outside world.
51. Describe the corvée system. What sort of work? At what time of year? How did you feel?
52. If known, describe falling into slavery, life as a slave, what production did slaves do?
53. Describe sending produce taxes to the state. What products did your village have to send as taxes—rice, forest goods etc? What proportion of total production?
54. Describe relations between the urban market and the village.
55. Describe relations between tax-farmers and the village.
56. What effects have changes in the outside world had on the village? Did commerce affect the structure of production and classes in the village? Was the effect good or bad, and in what ways? How did the village adjust to these changes?

57. Describe any gambling, opium-smoking, and crime which took place.
58. Has anyone from the village taken up a permanent occupation outside the village? Doing what? Labour or trading or what? What relations do they have with the village?
59. Describe any belief system or religion which came into the village from the outside world. Did the new system of belief affect old beliefs or not? How?

## Part 7. Questions about important events in the village

60. In your village, were there any important events or changes—for instance, new production methods, droughts, disasters, appearance of holy men and holy men revolts, etc.? When did each of these events take place? How did the event come about? How did the village adjust to the event? Why did it adjust or not adjust? Did these events cause any permanent changes in the village or not?

# APPENDIX 2

## DETAILS OF INTERVIEWEES

Name, age, address of interviewees and date of interviews.
Ages given as of the date of interview.

| | | SEX | AGE | ADDRESS | TAMBON | AMPHOE | PROVINCE | DATE |
|---|---|---|---|---|---|---|---|---|
| **CENTRAL REGION** | | | | | | | | |
| C:1 | Krod Oonlamai | M | 66 | 34 mu 5 | Hin Pak | Ban Mi | Lopburi | 23-Mar-82 |
| C:2 | Kimluan Phayapcharoen | M | 75 | | Samrong | Bang Khla | Chachoengsao | 26-Nov-78 |
| C:3 | Kamchon Wichitphan | M | 68 | Thasaophanit shop, 474/10 Samrancheun Rd | Thasao | Muang | Uttaradit | 25-Apr-83 |
| C:4 | Khachon Wangsuk | M | 78 | mu 1 | Chaksi | Muang | Singburi | 25-Mar-82 |
| C:5 | Khian Duangkham | M | 60 | mu 2 | Khunkhlon | Phraphutthabat | Saraburi | 26-Mar-82 |
| C:6 | Chamnian Tongrak | M | 63 | 22 mu 1 | Chaksi | Muang | Singburi | 5-Mar-82 |
| C:7 | Chamlong Sila | M | 60 | Ban Tako, 5 mu 5 | Khubua | Muang | Ratchaburi | 18-Feb-82 |
| C:8 | Chuang Amtrakun | M | 79 | Ban Latchado, 21 mu 5 | Nong Nam Yai | Phak Hai | Ayutthaya | 30-Mar-81 |
| C:9 | Chai Sawaengwuthitham | M | 83 | 525-7 | Khao Namtok | Laplae | Uttaradit | 25-Apr-82 |
| C:10 | Chun Chittarak | M | 77 | 37 mu 2 | Pakai | Paktho | Ratchaburi | 18-Feb-82 |
| C:11 | Sun Sae-tang | M | 80 | 2 mu 8 | Hin Pak | Ban Mi | Lopburi | 23-Mar-82 |
| C:12 | Son Khumha | M | 66 | 3 mu 5 | Chombung | Chombung | Ratchaburi | 15-Feb-82 |
| C:13 | Thongdaeng Wilathong | M | 74 | mu 5 | Chombung | Chombung | Ratchaburi | 15-Feb-82 |

| | | SEX | AGE | ADDRESS | TAMBON | AMPHOE | PROVINCE | DATE |
|---|---|---|---|---|---|---|---|---|
| C:14 | Thongdaeng Choeichom | M | 79 | 39 mu 7 | Khanmak | Muang | Lopburi | 26-Mar-82 |
| C:15 | Thot Khamkhae | M | 70 | 872 Samranrun Rd | Tha-it | Muang | Uttaradit | 25-Apr-83 |
| C:16 | Than Lumklun | M | 54 | 3 mu 5 | Chombung | Chombung | Ratchaburi | 15-Feb-82 |
| C:17 | Thongdi Charoenwat | M | | mu 6 | Tha Chang | Nakhon Luang | Ayutthaya | 12-Sep-81 |
| C:18 | Nikhom Suphanphaibun | M | 70 | 4 mu 6 | | Krokphra | Nakhon Sawan | 9-Dec-79 |
| C:19 | Bua Hema | M | 65 | 016/1 | | Tha Rua | Ayutthaya | 29-Mar-82 |
| C:20 | Prayong Sutthiprasoet | F | 31 | mu 5 | Amarit | Phak Hai | Ayutthaya | 30-Mar-82 |
| C:21 | Pun Siriphong | M | 65 | 4 mu 3 | Hin Pak | Ban Mi | Lopburi | 23-Mar-82 |
| C:22 | Puan Klinfung | M | 79 | 15 mu 2 | Pakai | Paktho | Ratchaburi | 18-Feb-82 |
| C:23 | Pluang & Lamai Phukniam | | 90 | Nong Tao | | Kao Lieo | Nakhon Sawan | 1-Dec-79 |
| C:24 | Pao Bua-ubon | M | 67 | mu 2 | Buachum | Chaibadan | Lopburi | 24-Mar-82 |
| C:25 | Pao Yongyun | M | 80 | 1 mu 1 | Chaibadan | Chombung | Lopburi | 15-Feb-82 |
| C:26 | Phuang Homchan | F | 66 | mu 5 | Chombung | Chombung | Ratchaburi | 15-Feb-82 |
| C:27 | Phrom Khumha | M | 66 | 11 mu 2 | Khonkhlang | Damnoen Saduak | Ratchaburi | 12-Feb-82 |
| C:28 | Phairot Khongmalai | M | 65 | Dara Furniture and Thai Silk | | Muang | Suphanburi | 4-Jun-83 |
| C:29 | Phim Rakprayun | F | | mu 6 | Tha Chang | Nakhon Luang | Ayutthaya | 12-Sep-81 |
| C:30 | Phrom Klaewkasikam | M | 97 | mu 6 | Lad Yao | Lad Yao | Nakhon Sawan | 9-Aug-79 |
| C:31 | Phuang Sopharat | F | 69 | Samrong | Bang Khla | Chachoengsao | 25-Nov-78 | |
| C:32 | Capt.. Man Wilawan | M | 76 | 056 Tha Rua Tha rd | Tha Lan | Tha Rua | Ayutthaya | 29-Mar-82 |
| C:33 | Maharot | | | 156 mu 3 | | Krokphra | Nakhon Sawan | 9-Dec-79 |
| C:34 | Acharn Monthian Dithae | | | Uttaradit Teachers College | | Muang | Uttaradit | 25-Apr-83 |
| C:35 | Mali Rakyat | F | 52 | 34 Mu 4 | Hin Pak | Ban Mi | Lopburi | 23-Mar-82 |
| C:36 | Roengrak Srikichakan | F | 50 | Bang sor market, mu 3 | Bang Tathen | Songphinong | Suphanburi | 5-Jun-83 |
| C:37 | Mangkon Chumthong | M | 50 | Ban Talunglek | Talunglek | Khok Samrong | Lopburi | 1 |
| C:38 | Lamun Suphanet | M | 74 | 34/1 | Phak Hai | Phak Hai | Ayutthaya | 30-Mar-82 |

| | | SEX | AGE | ADDRESS | TAMBON | AMPHOE | PROVINCE | DATE |
|---|---|---|---|---|---|---|---|---|
| C:39 | Lamiat Mangkhlaseni | M | 66 | 205 Prawet Nue | | Bang Munnak | Phichit | 27-Apr-83 |
| C:40 | Loetrit Sri | M | | 447 Behind railway station | | Tha Rua | Ayutthaya | 29-Mar-82 |
| C:41 | Lamom Sawetbongkot | F | 50 | Ban Nong Bua, 15 Mu 4 | | Chombung | Ratchaburi | 17-Feb-82 |
| C:42 | Lang Anantho | F | 74 | 2 Muban Nong Bua | | Chombung | Ratchaburi | 17-Feb-82 |
| C:43 | Lai (Kasem) Chalothon | M | | 24 Amarit | | Phak Hai | Ayutthaya | 30-Mar-81 |
| C:44 | Lamom Phamonsut | F | 84 | Wat Chonglom | | Muang | Ratchaburi | 16-Mar-82 |
| C:45 | Wanida Panphong | F | | 79/2 Ban Samthong | Talingchan | Muang | Suphanburi | 6-Jun-83 |
| C:46 | Khun Wiwonsukwithaya (Huang Lohawanit) | M | 80 | 4 Suchada rd | | Muang | Nakhon Sawan | 8-Dec-79 |
| C:47 | Wirat Theparak | M | 52 | Thepsahakit rice mill | 216 Suranarai | Samrong | Lopburi | 24-Mar-82 |
| C:48 | Winyu Patchamaphirom | M | 79 | Phichitphan rice mill, 20/1 Phraphichit Rd | | Muang | Phichit | 26-Apr-83 |
| C:49 | Khun Sikhonphumathikan | M | 90 | 68 Mu 4 | Bang Rachan | Bang Rachan | Singburi | 25-Mar-82 |
| C:50 | Phra Srithammanusat | | | Abbot of Wat Suriyawong | | Muang | Ratchaburi | 16-Feb-82 |
| C:51 | Son Kretkaew | M | 79 | 28 Mu 5 | Bang Takian | Song Phinong | Suphanburi | 5-Jun-83 |
| C:52 | Sangiam Charoensin | M | 76 | 358 Malaimaen Rd | | Muang | Suphanburi | 6-Jun-83 |
| C:53 | Hui Klangphet | M | 57 | 124/26 | Ratkasem rd | Muang | Phichit | 26-Apr-83 |
| C:54 | Maechi Nu Pilanon | F | 68 | Muban Saladaeng | Sam Khok | Sam Khok | Pathumthani | 20-Feb-79 |
| C:55 | Nai Sathuphan | F | 83 | 88 mu 1, Ban Samthong | Talingchan | Muang | Suphanburi | 6-Jun-83 |
| C:56 | Akhom Chatuphon | M | | Chatuphon store, 133-5 Phraram rd | Chaolang | Muang | Lopburi | 26-Mar-82 |
| C:57 | Iam Ditcharoen | M | | 24 mu 4 | Hin Pak | Ban Mi | Lopburi | 23-Mar-82 |
| C:58 | Iam Thavon | M | 71 | 778 Khoksala | Tha Rua | Tha Rua | Ayutthaya | 29-Mar-82 |
| C:59 | Udom Chittrathon | M | 60 | 196 Khwae Yai | | Muang | Nakhon Sawan | 8-Dec-79 |
| C:60 | Aram Chuangsuwanit | F | 59 | 352 Petkasem Rd | Na Muang | Muang | Ratchaburi | 16-Feb-82 |
| C:61 | Anonymous | ? | 72 | 166 Maensri Rd 2 | | Bamrungmuang | Bangkok | 1-Jun-79 |

| | | SEX | AGE | ADDRESS | TAMBON | AMPHOE | PROVINCE | DATE |
|---|---|---|---|---|---|---|---|---|
| **NORTH** | | | | | | | | |
| N:62 | Kimho Nimmanhemin | F | 84 | 36 Thaphae Rd | | Muang | Chiang Mai | 20-Feb-79 |
| N:63 | Phrakhru Chan Chanthathammo | | | | | Samoeng | Chiang Mai | 23-Feb-79 |
| N:64 | Khamna Upayo | M | 80 | 17 mu 5 | Samoeng Tai | Samoeng | Chiang Mai | |
| N:65 | Khow Hang Yin | | | Wat U-mong | | Muang | Chiang Mai | 18-Feb-79 |
| N:66 | Chao Khruakaew na Chiang Mai | F | 68 | Chiang Mai College of Dance | | Muang | Chiang Mai | 13-Dec-79 [2] |
| N:67 | Khampaeng Aphiwong | M | 74 | | | Sanpatong | Chiang Mai | 30-Jul-79 [2] |
| N:68 | Chia Nitu | M | 96 | km.150 Chiang Mai/Chiang Rai Rd | | Wiangpapao | Chiang Rai | 28-Dec-81 |
| N:69 | Chao Chang Yonghuai | M | | interviewed at Chiang Mai Teachers College | | Muang | Chiang Mai | 26-Dec-81 |
| N:70 | Chao Chun Sirorot | M | | Wat U-mong | | Muang | Chiang Mai | 18-Feb-79 |
| N:71 | Tit Tankai | M | 54 | Ban Phae | | Thungchang | Nan | 31-Dec-81 |
| N:72 | Chao Nop Mahawongnan | M | | | | Muang | Nan | 31-Dec-81 |
| N:73 | Pan Chaiwong | M | | U-mong village | | Muang | Chiang Mai | 18-Feb-79 |
| N:74 | Phenchai Sirorot | F | 52 | Wat U-mong | | Muang | Chiang Mai | 24-Jun-82 |
| N:75 | Phumin Chaemchit | M | 70 | mu 4 | Nong Yaeng | Sansai | Chiang Mai | |
| N:76 | Luangpho Ma (Pat Patama) | M | 96 | | | Samoeng | Chiang Mai | 23-Sep-79 |
| N:77 | Yun Kaewphuangthong | M | 66 | 64 mu 3 | Wiang Yong | Muang | Lamphun | |
| N:78 | Phra Srithammanitet | M | 80 | Wat Sanpakhoi | | Muang | Chiang Mai | 23-Feb-79 |
| N:79 | Somkiat Phuprasoet | M | | 191 Chiang Mai/Chiang Rai Rd | | Wiangpapao | Chiang Rai | 28-Dec-81 |
| N:80 | Chao Inthanon na Chiang Mai | M | 69 | 104 Maninaphrat Rd | | Muang | Chiang Mai | 13-Dec-79 [2] |
| **SOUTH** | | | | | | | | |
| S:81 | Kluan Sirinuphong | M | 76 | 232-4 mu 4, Soiwari Rd | | Ranot | Songkhla | 10-Jan-80 |
| S:82 | Kluan Phaendet | M | 70 | mu 1 | Chalong | Sichon | Nakhon Sithammarat | |
| S:83 | Pol. Maj.-Gen. Khun Phantharakratchadet | | | 764/5 Soi Ratchakon | Klang | Muang | Nakhon Sithammarat | 13-Jan-80 |
| S:84 | Chaeng Bunyaman | M | 90 | 95 Nang Ngam Rd | | Muang | Songkhla | 9-Jan-80 |

| | | SEX | AGE | ADDRESS | TAMBON | AMPHOE | PROVINCE | DATE |
|---|---|---|---|---|---|---|---|---|
| S:84 | Chaeng Bunyaman | M | 90 | 95 Nang Ngam Rd | | Muang | Songkhla | 9-Jan-80 |
| S:85 | Charat Upla | F | 74 | 1 mu 7 | Nalae | Chawang | Nakhon Sithammarat | |
| S:86 | U Angsuphanit | F | | 76-8 Satunthani Rd | | Muang | Satun | 3-May-83 |
| S:87 | Chua Kankaew | M | 72 | 354 Donnok Rd | | Muang | Surat Thani | 22-Jan-84 |
| S:88 | Chun Trachu | M | 72 | 33 mu 2 | Chang Klang | Chawang | Nakhon Sithammarat | |
| S:89 | Se Sonsamet | F | | | | Chaiya | Surat Thani | 21-Feb-80 |
| S:90 | Chamnan Matla | M | 62 | Ban Natap, 67 mu 7 | Tha Sala | Tha Sala | Nakhon Sithammarat | |
| S:91 | Seng Srisuchat | F | mu 4 | | Sa Kaew | Tha Sala | Nakhon Sithammarat | 22-Jan-82 |
| S:92 | Decho Bunchuai | M | 56 | Malini Nursery School, km. 3 | | Muang | Surat Thani | 22-Jan-80 |
| S:93 | Duan Kanchanaphen | M | 67 | mu 7 | Chumphon | Thingphra | Songkhla | |
| S:94 | Montri Ratchamani | M | 60 | mu 5, Ban Mai | Phipun | Phipun | Nakhon Sithammarat | |
| S:95 | Thap Chaimongkon | M | 79 | mu 2 | Chumphon | Thingphra | Songkhla | |
| S:96 | Thani Phairotpak | M | 46 | 14/1 mu 9 | Ko Yo | Muang | Songkhla | |
| S:97 | Nin Suntharanon | M | 86 | 2 Sukphonrat | | Yantakhao | Trang | 3-May-83 |
| S:98 | Bun Wandao | M | 55 | 038 mu 4 | Khok Phrabat | Chian Yai | Nakhon Sithammarat | |
| S:99 | Bamrung Chaisamut | M | 69 | 89 mu 2 | Tha Kham | Palian | Trang | |
| S:100 | Plaek Silpakampiset | M | | 80 Thale Luang rd | Bo Yang | Muang | Songkhla | 7-Jan-80 |
| S:101 | Phokin Anantaphan | M | 63 | 26 mu 6 | | Ko Yo | Songkhla | 9-Jan-80 |
| S:102 | Fak Ratanasombat | M | 72 | 1 mu 5 | Sra Kaew | Tha Sala | Nakhon Sithammarat | |
| S:103 | Phlang Talungchit | M | 73 | 124 mu 1 | Tha Di | Lan Saka | Nakhon Sithammarat | |
| S:104 | Phua Chai-ari | M | 73 | 1 mu 5 | Thung Prang | Sichon | Nakhon Sithammarat | |
| S:105 | Phloi Kaewmani | F | 92 | Ban Nong Muang, mu 7 | Prik | Thung Yai | Nakhon Sithammarat | |
| S:106 | Maen Hanumat | M | 53 | 17 mu 3 | Lan Saka | Lan Saka | Nakhon Sithammarat | |
| S:107 | Acharn Mano Khambamrung | | | Phuket Teachers College | | Muang | Phuket | 5-Mar-80 |

| | | SEX | AGE | ADDRESS | TAMBON | AMPHOE | PROVINCE | DATE |
|---|---|---|---|---|---|---|---|---|
| S:108 | Yisae Bontaban | M | 80 | 63 Srithammarat rd | | Muang | Nakhon Sithammarat | 15-Jan-80 |
| S:109 | Yuti Bawonrattanarak | M | 67 | Bawonphanit Co. Ltd. | | Muang | Nakhon Sithammarat | 14-Jan-80 |
| S:110 | Wichit Kanchanasuwan | M | 44 | 097 Pak Phanang market | | Pak Phanang | Nakhon Sithammarat | 15-Jan-80 |
| S:111 | Wichai Sawatdinarunat | M | | Mayor of Pak Phanang | | Pak Phanang | Nakhon Sithammarat | 15-Jan-80 |
| S:112 | Phra Ratchasinsangwon (Chuang Ruangnu) | | 78 | Wat Matchimawat | | | Songkhla | 2-Jun-05 |
| S:113 | Sengiam Srichanthong | M | | 84 mu 4 | Mai Fat | Sikao | Trang | 5-May-83 |
| S:114 | Somsak Adithepworaphan | M | | 549 Ratchadamnoen Rd | | Muang | Nakhon Sithammarat | 14-Jan-80 |
| S:115 | Suchat Rattanaprakan | M | 71 | 65 Nakhon Nai Rd | | Muang | Songkhla | 11-Jan-80 |
| S:116 | Matsen Rattanatrang | M | 101 | 45 mu 4, Ban Nala | Mai Fat | Sikao | Trang | |
| S:117 | Mi Srichanthong | M | 61 | 7 mu 1 | Khao Wiset | Wang Wiset | Trang | |
| S:118 | Khun Athetkhadi (Klon Manlikamat) | M | 93 | 203 Thasi Rd | | Muang | Nakhon Sithammarat | 14-Jan-80 |
| S:119 | Na-a Phongyuso | M | 95 | 91 Phalang Phrathat Rd | | Muang | Nakhon Sithammarat | 15-Jan-80 |
| S:120 | An Plotthong | M | 74 | 43 mu 1 | Ko Yo | Muang | Songkhla | |
| S:121 | Uthai Kitikhun | M | 57 | 383 Chaiwari Rd | | Ranot | Songkhla | 10-Jan-80 |
| **ISAN** | | | | | | | | |
| I:122 | Khwan Sae Tan | M | 68 | 266 Chaikhong Rd | | Chiang Khan | Loei | 15-Jul-793 |
| I:123 | Khai Lapbunruang | M | 73 | Ban Dongnoi, 14 mu 3 | Huai Pho | Muang | Kalasin | |
| I:124 | Kham Wongchali | M | 65 | Ban Kho 49 | Nong Chik | Borabu | Mahasarakham | |
| I:125 | Khamdi Rattanamun | M | 99 | Ban Kaeng Tai, 99 mu 4 | Muang Yai | Khemmarat | Ubon Ratchathani | |
| I:126 | Khamphan Buami | F | 90 | 82 Sri Chiangkhan Rd | | Chiang Khan | Loei | 29-Dec-79 |
| I:127 | Khamphan Khwakuphan | M | 70 | 147 mu 1 | Kusuman | Kusuman | Sakon Nakhon | |
| I:128 | Khamsing Inpiya | M | 63 | 44 Thatwithi | | Renu Nakhon | Nakhon Phanom | 5-Jan-803 |
| I:129 | Khamla Sonphim | M | 54 | 54 mu 11 | Na Kaew | Muang | Sakon Nakhon | |

| | | SEX | AGE | ADDRESS | TAMBON | AMPHOE | PROVINCE | DATE |
|---|---|---|---|---|---|---|---|---|
| I:130 | Charoen Hangkrathok | F | 38 | 85 mu 1, Ban Mai Thai Charoen | Saraphi | Chokchai | Korat3 | |
| I:131 | Chali Rattanaphon | M | 62 | Ban Chiang Hian, 182 mu 3 | Khewa | Muang | Mahasarakham | |
| I:132 | Duang Karik | M | 60 | 142 mu 4 | Tha Bo | Srisongkhram | Nakhon Phanom | |
| I:133 | Da Khamnuk | M | 72 | Ban Donkha, 44 mu 5 | Phran | Khunhan | Sisaket | |
| I:134 | Di Luamsi | M | 103 | Ban Chat, 91 mu 4 | Nakhu | Khaowong | Kalasin | |
| I:135 | Taeng Chimpli | F | | 318 mu 6 | Kusuman | Kusuman | Sakon Nakhon | 25-Feb-82 |
| I:136 | Taem Than-ngam | F | 70 | Ban Donkha, mu 5 | Phran | Khunhan | Sisaket | |
| I:137 | Tan Yotpanya | M | | Ban Na Pung, mu 1 | | | Loei | 15-Jul-82 |
| I:138 | Thonglang Manta | M | | 74/82 Phanomphanarak Rd | | That Phanom | Nakhon Phanom | |
| I:139 | Thong Sobun | M | | Ban Chiang Khrua 66 | Chiang Khrua | Muang | Sakon Nakhon | 13-Nov-80 |
| I:140 | Thunchit Khatiphot | F | 60 | 1566 Kamchatphai Rd | | Muang | Sakon Nakhon | 12-Nov-80 |
| I:141 | Thum Nawa | F | | 2457 Ban Nawa Tai | | Phoisai | Ubon Ratchathani | 16-Mar-83 |
| I:142 | Thongsi Phonruang | F | 69 | Ban Dongnoi, 58 mu 3 | Huay Pho | Muang | Kalasin | |
| I:143 | Thongdi Saenkhamphumi | F | 68 | Ban Nangyai 1802 | Muang | Muang | Mahasarakham | |
| I:144 | Nut Wongphanawan | M | 55 | 214 mu 4 | | Nakae | Nakhon Phanom | 28-Sep-82 |
| I:145 | Buadi Thatanam | M | | 10 mu 3 | Samrong | Khemmarat | Ubon Ratchathani | 15-Mar-83 |
| I:146 | Bunloet Ketkaewmani | M | 76 | 1 Phumwithi rd | | Wang | Loei | 19-Jul-80 |
| I:147 | Bunhuat Ittarat | M | 60 | 1285 Charoen Ratchadet 2 | | Muang | Mahasarakham | 4-Mar-82 |
| I:148 | Pe Supsuk | M | 81 | Ban Nawa Tai, 7 mu 3 | | Phosai | Ubon Ratchathani | 15-Apr-83 |
| I:149 | Phon Choknat | M | 65 | 30 mu 6, Ban Saothongyai | | Trakan | Ubon Ratchathani | 6-Jan-80 |
| I:150 | Phan Bunsuk | F | 66 | mu 3 | Ko-che | Khuan Nai | Ubon Ratchathani | |
| I:151 | Phrom Hawong | M | 83 | 12 mu 3, Ban Nawa Tai | Samrong | Khemmarat | Ubon Ratchathani | |
| I:152 | Phin Atthasit | M | 82 | 3038 Trok Pa Mai | | Muang | Korat | 5-Aug-79 |

| | | SEX | AGE | ADDRESS | TAMBON | AMPHOE | PROVINCE | DATE |
|---|---|---|---|---|---|---|---|---|
| I:153 | Phi Sinchai | F | 82 | 104 mu 5 | Chang Yai | Muang Samsip | Ubon Ratchathani | |
| I:154 | Phim Saenghao | F | | 15 Ban Nong Khuan Chang | Tha Song Don | Muang | Mahasarakham | |
| I:155 | Fong Nuanmani | M | 84 | | | Muang | Sakon Nakhon | |
| I:156 | Ma Prasoetsuk | M | 83 | 43 Sirat Rd | | Muang | Loei | 13-Jul-79 |
| I:157 | Ma Chamnanwet | F | 68 | 941 mu 5 | Nong Chang | Muang Samsip | Ubon Ratchathani | |
| I:158 | Loi Chatchawan | M | | Ban Na-o, 27 mu 10 | Na-o | Muang | Loei | 18-Jul-79 |
| I:159 | Luang Pho Loeng Khamna | M | 70 | Wat Nonsai, | Puanphu | Phukradung | Loei | |
| I:160 | La Choemthonglang | F | 68 | mu 1, Ban Mai Thai Charoen | Saraphi | Chokchai | Korat | |
| I:161 | Acharn Wirat Butsayakun | | | 598 Sakon Nakhon/Udon Rd | Phang Khwang | Muang | Sakon Nakhon | 1-Mar-82 |
| I:162 | Wisit & Praphin Wattanasuchat | | | 1353/2 Sukkhasem Rd | | Muang | Sakon Nakhon | 11-Nov-80 |
| I:163 | Wong Lachai | M | 74 | Ban Nong Krabok, 119 mu 11 | Na Kaew | Muang | Sakon Nakhon | |
| I:164 | Sat Phromsakha na Sakon Nakhon | | | Muang municipality | | Muang | Sakon Nakhon | 18-Nov-80 |
| I:165 | Somsi Wongkraso | M | 103 | Ban Dong Luang, 89 mu 3 | Dong Luang | Dong Luang | Nakhon Phanom | |
| I:166 | Satcha Thanaprakop | M | 52 | Korat rice mill, 125 mu 2 | Ban Ko | Muang | Korat | |
| I:167 | San Sarathatnanan | M | 63 | 16 soi 1, Sakon Chiang Khan rd | Muang | Loei | | 16-Jul-79 |
| I:168 | Si Kingsi | M | 70 | Ban Pak Chong, 15 mu 9 | Koktum | Dong Luang | Nakhon Phanom | |
| I:169 | Sing Thumsongkhram | M | 101 | Ban That, 37 Mu 2 | | Chiang Khan | Loei | 18-Jul-79 |
| I:170 | Sing Phungok | M | 69 | Ban Nawa Tai | | Phosai | Ubon Ratchathani | 16-Mar-83 |
| I:171 | Sing Yuangchip | M | | Ban Sa-at, 14 mu 1 | Sa-at | Nam Phong | Khon Kaen | 2-Mar-82 |
| I:172 | Sunthon Baiphasi | M | 43 | 101 mu 2 | Kusuman | Kusuman | Sakon Nakhon | |
| I:173 | Som Phraphutthachat | F | 59 | Ban Sapu | | Trakan | Ubon Ratchathani | 31-Dec-79 |

| | | SEX | AGE | ADDRESS | TAMBON | AMPHOE | PROVINCE | DATE |
|---|---|---|---|---|---|---|---|---|
| I:174 | Sophi Rattana-saengsuksakan | F | | | | Muang | Mahasarakham | 10-Jul-79 |
| I:175 | Nuphin Kosanwat | F | 70 | Rungruang store, Luang Rd | | Phibun- | Ubon Ratchathani | 28-Dec-79 |
| I:176 | Mot (surname unknown) | F | 83 | Ban Pong, mu 3 | Muang Yai | Khemmarat | Ubon Ratchathani | |
| I:177 | Yong Namsuwan | F | 65 | 21 mu 4, Ban Non Yai | Ko-che | Khuan Nai | Ubon Ratchathani | |
| I:178 | Hui Sirichinda | M | 62 | Chaipruek Rice mill, 147/2 Suranarai Rd | | Muang | Korat | 5-Aug-79 |
| I:179 | Luk Chairin | M | 69 | Ban Nong Ba Thao, 42 mu 2 Srisongkhram | | Muang | Sakon Nakhon | |
| I:180 | Onsi Phuaphutanon na Mahasarakham | F | 81 | 92 Charoen Ratchadet Rd 2 | | Muang | Mahasarakham | 3-Jul-82 [3] |
| I:181 | Udom Makarawet | M | | Thai Udom Hotel | | Muang | Loei | 16-Jul-82 |
| I:182 | Hao Thepsittha | M | | Ban Saphu, 15 mu 4 | Saphu | Trakan | Ubon Ratchathani | 31-Dec-79 |

1 Interviewed by student at Thepsatri Teachers College

2 Interviewed by Chusit Chuchat

3 Interviewed by Phranut Sapphayasan

# AFTERWORD: CHATTHIP AND THE THAI VILLAGE

The theme of *The Thai Village Economy in the Past* appears very simple: the Thai rural economy in the past was a subsistence economy, and this subsistence economy survived until much later than most would expect—until the turn of this century in the central plain, and until around the Second World War in other regions.

The telling of the story is also deceptively simple. The text of the original publication ran to just ninety-five pages. The writing is almost completely free of academic jargon. Much of the text is taken up with description of ploughs, fish-traps, weaving, pounding rice, and spirit ceremonies. Only in one short passage does Chatthip refer to another contemporary academic author (Nithi Eosiwong).

In a seminar on the book's first appearance in 1984, one colleague questioned why a Thai historian needed to write a book describing how Thai farmers grew rice, caught fish, gathered from the forests, and wove cloth. Surely everyone knew all this. Maybe some foreigners might be interested but for Thais the content was commonplace.

Yet the message and meaning of the book have proved to be far from simple.

Foreigners have certainly been interested. A Japanese translation was published in 1986. A Chinese version is under preparation. Many Western academics have read, cited, and commented on the book's content. But the book has also had a powerful and lasting appeal in Thailand. Fifteen years after its first appearance, it is still in print. Much of the appeal stems from some of its simple but startling ideas. The village existed before capitalism and before the state. The village has its own culture which is different from that of city and state. Buddhism came from outside and had to compromise with local beliefs. Households, villages, and localities have their own spirits, but the Thai state does not.

*The Thai Village Economy in the Past* contains ideas which continue to excite supporters and critics many years after its first appearance. This afterword provides some background material to help in understanding the book and its importance.

## CHATTHIP'S BACKGROUND AND CAREER

Chatthip Nartsupha comes from a Bangkok upper-middle-class background. On his father's side, his grandfather was a judge, and his grandmother was a minor member of the royal family. His mother's side is related to a Chiang Mai noble family (Chao Chuen Sirorot), and his mother's father was also a minor member of the royal family. His father was a medical doctor with a military rank, and several other relatives work as professionals in academic and high civil service positions.

Chatthip was educated in Bangkok, studied for a B.A. in political science at Chulalongkorn University, and then went to Tufts University where he completed his doctorate in 1968 with a dissertation on "Foreign Trade, Foreign Finance and the Economic Development of Thailand, 1959–1965". He returned to take up a teaching post in the economics faculty at Chulalongkorn.

During the course of this education, three people played key roles in shaping Chatthip's view of the world. At Triam Udom school, Prawut Srimantra taught him English and also introduced him to humanitarian socialist ideas, particularly through the works of Siburapha and Seni Saowaphong. At Chulalongkorn University, Wichitwong Na Pomphet taught him economics and stirred his interest in Thai history. Wichitwong is related to Pridi Banomyong, a leader of the 1932 revolution, and has written an important biography of Pridi. While studying at Tufts, Woraphut Chaiyanam, a fellow student and voracious reader, introduced Chatthip to anarchist ideas, particularly the writings of Kropotkin.

Since the early 1970s, Chatthip's influence on Thai social science has been remarkable for its breadth and its depth. He has written at least three books which are among the most read, referenced, and quoted in the past generation of Thai social science research. He is one of very few Thai academics whose name and work is well known outside the country. He has played a major part in establishing three schools of study—the political economy group at Chulalongkorn University, the school of village study based on a cultural approach, and a new social and cultural study of Tai communities across the region. Each of these phases has projected a wave of new researchers and teachers into the academic community. He was chosen by the National Research Council as the most outstanding researcher (*nak wichai diden haeng chat*) of the year for 1983. He has been awarded the prestigious title of senior research scholar (*methi wichai awuso*). He has been selected among a small group of modern Thai thinkers for critical review in a project of the Thailand Research Fund.

That much is simply the career pattern of a good university professor. But Chatthip's influence stretches beyond the university and outside the bounds of academe. Although he is based in the Faculty of Economics, his students, followers and collaborators are scattered through the Faculties of History, Literature, Philosophy, Anthropology, Political Science, and Linguistics. Although his career has been based in Chulalongkorn University, he has a dense network of colleagues through the provincial campuses, the teachers' colleges, secondary schools, and NGO workers all over the country. On the Tai project, he has built a network which stretches across India, Laos, Vietnam, and China.

## CHATTHIP'S WORK

One of Chatthip's academic ambitions has been to construct "a theory of social science for Thai society" (*thritsadi sangkhomsat thai*). According to

Chatthip, there must be a new explanation of social phenomena which is distinctively Thai, based on a distinctly Thai theoretical approach to social science.

It is often observed by others (and admitted by Chatthip himself), that his work falls into two parts. First he studied Thai economic history. Later he turned to the study of Thai village culture. The two volumes of *The Political Economy of Siam* written with Suthy Prasartset are the major work of the first phase. *The Thai Village Economy in the Past* is the seminal work of the second.

The unifying theme of these two phases has been Chatthip's interest in the "little people" and their role in Thai history. To understand this interest properly, we need to recall the role of history and historiography in modern Thai culture. History was one of the major tools which the modern Thai state used to legitimate its existence, to dazzle its subjects, and to enforce their loyalty. From the early years of the Rattanakosin dynasty, the rulers devoted considerable efforts to finding, compiling, editing, and publishing works on the pre-history and history of the region which became Siam and then Thailand. This history served two key roles. First, it provided a legitimating link between the new Bangkok dynasty and centuries of royal history stretching back to Sukhothai and beyond. Second, it portrayed a society divided starkly between "lords of life" on the one hand, and powerless, dutiful subjects on the other.

When a new generation in the 1970s set out to overthrow the old-style state, they also set out to overthrow the old-style history which the state had constructed. For many, this was to be done by rescuing the little people from their passive, subjected role in that history. Often the vehicle for this reorientation of history was Marxism, or more exactly the Marxist dialectic which, as Craig Reynolds and Lysa Hong noted, served as "a lever to pry the chronicles and archives away from royalist and nationalist myth-making concerns".[1] Some of these new historians, like Jit Phumisak, were interested in explaining the deep roots of the Thai state's domination. Chatthip was more interested in the way the modern state exploited and suppressed the little people, how the little people resisted, and how this resistance might lead to the overthrow of exploitation and suppression. In this period, as Chatthip himself notes, his primary interest was the state.

Although his work in this phase (roughly 1972 to 1981) was concerned with the little people as the objects of exploitation, the angle of vision was clearly top-down. While his work challenged the image of the state (benign, progressive, glorious) in traditional Thai historiography, his work still implicitly confirmed that the chief role of history was tracing the genealogy of the state.

In many countries historians have confronted this same dilemma—that studying the state, even from a critical perspective, tends to magnify the state's importance. They have looked around for ways to switch the focus of history from the state to the people. Often this search has led to histories of resistance, and of the culture of resistance. Prominent examples are the school of English historiography associated with E. P. Thompson, the studies of the crowd by French and other continental historians, some of the work of the Annales school, and the subaltern studies school in colonial history. All these approaches continue to focus on the struggle between oppressor and oppressed at the core of the Marxist dialectic. But they differ by focusing clearly on the oppressed, and by looking bottom-up rather than top-down.

In the early 1980s, Chatthip shifted his focus of study from the state to the village. As he explained,

> I was just like other social scientists [in the 1970s]. Everyone studied the state. There were many books and articles on the subject. We were not conscious that we were following the crowd. It was the agenda of "Thai studies" at the time. But Achan Suthy [Prasartset] and I were different from others in that we studied the Thai state and then we rejected it. After rejecting it, we had to confront what to do next. I wanted to look at what is the core of Thai society, what is the goodness of Thai society. My interest in Thai villages came in this way. I came to study Thai villages after I studied the Thai state and rejected it. Scholars like Achan Srisak Vallipodom also studied villages but he did not reject the state. In my

case I began with studying the state and then rejected it. (Interview, 11 October 1996)

Chatthip's shift was critically different from the European models. After the polarisation and violence of 1975–76, there was a trend within the Thai left to move away from the politics of confrontation. In the realm of political organisation and strategy, this led to decline of Maoist or Leninist strategies of revolutionary struggle, the collapse of the Communist Party of Thailand (CPT), and the emergence of NGO movements which tried to avoid the state rather than challenge it.

In parallel, many leftist intellectuals working in Asia, both indigenous and foreign, cast around for new ways of thinking about the culture and politics of the local community. Among Western scholarly work on Asia, one of the best-known products of this era is James Scott's focus on "everyday forms of resistance"—ways in which villagers and other dominated people evade and cushion themselves against state power as part of the strategy of their everyday lives. Chatthip acknowledges the influence of Scott, but his approach has its own uniqueness.

When Chatthip embarked on studies of the village, his main focus was still on the state. He had been attracted to Marx's Asiatic Mode of Production as a way to explain that capitalism developed slowly in Asia because of obstruction from strong village communities. He started studying the village in order to learn how to overcome this obstruction and hence hasten the cycle of bourgeois and socialist revolutions. According to him,

I went into the villages to discover why villages are problematic. The Asiatic Mode of Production theory asserts that the village community is the obstacle to development towards capitalism. It explains why Asiatic society did not progress along the lines of capitalist Europe. I also found that there is a gap in the historical study on this question.

I was looking for villages which had the social character to develop capitalism from within. I wanted to understand why Thai villages, which were famous for craftsmen who produced things like knives, did not develop into centres of manufacturing. I was concerned that there should be a capitalism developed from inside Thai society and not imported from outside.

After I went into the villages I found the village community possessed its own goodness. I was impressed. I did not find that the village is the source of the problem. So I did not follow through with the Asiatic Mode of Production theory. I no longer saw the village community as an obstacle to change. I saw it as a potential force for change in parallel with the middle class. Earlier on, I saw the bourgeoisie as the only agent of change. After studying the villages I stressed village culture as a leading agent. I think both of them have roles. (Interview, 11 October 1996)

He rejected the view, inherent in both Marxist and many conservative philosophies, which sees the state as the agent of social progress. Instead, he started to see the value in the village community, and the threat which state and capitalism posed to the village community's existence. He rejected the idea of writing history which glorified the role of the state, and which could be used by the state as an instrument of hegemonic domination.

Most historians come from the city, work at universities in the city, and write about the growth and development of city-based cultures. When they peer out towards the villages, they tend to focus on the links which connect the village to the city, the city economy, and the city culture. In *The Thai Village Economy in the Past*, Chatthip wanted to swivel this angle of vision through a full 180 degrees. He set out to write the history of the village as seen from the village. He argued that from this perspective, the state was much less important than it appeared in conventional study. In effect his shift was like reversing a pair of binoculars: where the state once filled the foreground, now it was reduced to a distant speck. The village has its own history and culture—and its own consciousness of its history and culture—which exist totally independent from the pretensions and structures of the state. Studying this history and culture offers a corrective to the bias in favour of the state.

In the early 1980s, this approach represented a dramatic political statement. Over the six years that *The Thai Village Economy in the Past* was researched and written, the Mao-inspired vision of a rural-based revolution, so popular in the mid-1970s, crumbled away. The murderous nature of the Khmer Rouge was revealed. China backed away from support for rural movements in the region. The Thai students who had fled to the jungle in 1976 filtered back to the city, with several voicing public criticism of the CPT and its Maoist pro-peasant line. Under the policy of Order 66/2523, the Thai army clamped controls over the villages through vigilantes and propaganda organisations. Economists and businessmen looked to the East Asian Tigers for a very different model to revolutionise Thailand through urban-based industrialisation.

As a subject for study, a base for political activity, or a repository of hope for change, the Thai countryside was being wiped off the map. The subjects which would attract many new Thai historians over the next decade conspicuously avoided the countryside. These historians focused instead on the role of the urban Thai-Chinese, the nature of (urban) nationalism, and the growth of urban economies and cultures.

*The Thai Village Economy in the Past* stood out against this trend. Indeed, Chatthip's 180-degree pivot of the historian's standpoint was an implicit protest against the strengthening urban bias in the economy, politics, and intellectual outlook. This protest is not overtly argued in this book. Rather, it surfaces in the dedication and in the strong message of the book's final paragraph. In works written later, Chatthip set out his position very clearly. The village, he argued, has its own society and culture which are profoundly different from those of state and city. Providing the village with a history which emphasises this individuality is one small contribution to building the village culture's self-respect, self-confidence, and ability to survive.

## CHATTHIP AND THE CRITICS

Many critics of Chatthip and of *The Thai Village Economy in the Past* claim to reject the methodology (particularly the reliance on oral history) or the findings. In most cases their real objection is to the angle of vision and the politics it represents.

Some like Anan Ganjanaphan and Katherine Bowie[2] have pointed to the evidence for trade and specialised production to invalidate Chatthip's claim that the village economy was at base a subsistence economy. But Chatthip already anticipates this objection in the text. He does not deny the existence of craft production, local trade, and gathering of export products. Indeed he describes these processes in some detail. Yet he argues that the fundamental logic of the village economy, expressed in the means and relations of production and in the culture which underpinned them, was oriented to subsistence. Commercial exchange was a subsidiary activity which did not undermine this basic logic. Nobody argues that the modern Thai economy is subsistence rather than capitalist just because the government barter-trades rice for F-16s.

Jeremy Kemp, Atsui Kitahara, and others[3] have denied that the village could retain its own economy and culture when the village exists within a framework created by the state and the urban capitalist economy. Chatthip admits that under normal circumstances, these powerful forces would break down the smaller, weaker, and less advanced structures of the village. But, Chatthip argues, the Thai case was special. The state and export-trading economy were interested only in skimming a surplus out of the villages. They had no interest in interfering further to rearrange village production systems. There was no mechanism, similar to the role of landlords in other agrarian cultures, to act as an agent of change. Old Siam developed a radically dual economy.

Other critics are more explicit in rejecting Chatthip's view on theoretical or political grounds. Many are Marxists who continue to believe in the power of the dialectic, and in the political consequences which stem from it. Scott's work on everyday forms of resistance has attracted similar attacks. For example, Brass has argued that Scott's perspective takes the attention away from analysing the repressive power of the state, and down-weights the importance of organisa-tions created to challenge state power. Kemp's criticisms of Chatthip fall into the same vein, although Kemp does not make his own theoretical inclinations quite so clear.

Chatthip has also been accused of romanticising the village, and of taking a romantic, backward-looking view of the world which denies the benefits of urbanism, modernism, and "progress". The critics argue that Chatthip paints out the ugly side of village life—the short life-span, the petty cruelties of inward-looking communities, and most of all the simple hardships of survival—while ignoring the benefits of technology and urban liberal ideas. These criticisms have been voiced by Thais and westerners, but most sharply by Japanese scholars who find parallels between Chatthip's ideas and the rural focus of conservative strains in Japanese twentieth-century thought. Kitahara says clearly that he sees the state as a civilising and liberating force, and hence rejects Chatthip's focus on village autonomy.

Yet Chatthip accepts that the backwardness of the village was the root of its own downfall. He accepts the value of modern technology and also of liberal ideas. The main question posed by his work from *The Thai Village Economy in the Past* onwards has been how to achieve a synthesis between Western-based science and liberalism on the one hand, and the cooperative, humanistic social values of the village on the other.

The shift to a village-centred perspective has shaped Chatthip's acceptance within the academic community. He has tended to attract most criticism from historians and economists, both of whom work in disciplines which traditionally focus heavily on the role of the state. By contrast, he has tended to collect followers more easily in anthropology, linguistics, and cultural studies which are not so dominated by a state-centred perspective.[4] Similarly, he has often been criticised by the academies buried in the heart of the capital and in the heart of metropolitan culture, while he has had great appeal for many who work in the upcountry colleges and outside formal academic structures. His appeal spreads outside academic circles and reaches many who have an instinctive rejection of top-down modes of thought.

## BEYOND
## *THE THAI VILLAGE ECONOMY IN THE PAST*

Very soon after the first publication of *The Thai Village Economy in the Past* in 1984, the Thai economy entered a period of rapid change. For a decade, the economy grew at world-record pace. The growth was concentrated in the urban areas—especially Bangkok—while the rural economy stagnated. Driven by economic stagnation and often also ecological deterioration in the village, and drawn by rising employment demand and the attractions of urban culture, several million people migrated from village to city. Local communities were often damaged and distorted by this population movement. The balance between urban and rural in the economy, the society, and in the culture totally changed. Through rising exports, financial liberalisation, and better communications, society and economy were opened up more to the outside world.

Over this period since 1984, Chatthip has published three major blocks of work. First was a review of the "community culture" school of thought. This appeared in Thai in 1989 and in English in 1991.[5] Second was a series of works on Thai village culture, some co-authored with students and colleagues. These appeared between 1991 and 1997.[6] Third are the outputs of a broad-ranging study on "A Social and Cultural History of Tai Ethnic Communities". These have begun to appear since the mid-1990s.[7] Through this series, Chatthip has gradually moved further away from state and capitalism both in the focus of his research and his explanation of its political purpose.

In *The Thai Village Economy in the Past*, Chatthip seems to accept that twentieth-century capitalism has been an extraordinarily powerful force and that the grand theme of the century has been the triumph of the urban economy and culture. He is interested in the fate of rural culture precisely within this context. The old Thai rural economy, he concludes, lost out because it failed to develop its technology and its productive capacity. He contrasts the history of the west, where the rural economy developed through interplay with emerging urban capitalism, with the modern fate of poorer nations whose rural economies tend to crumble when they are abruptly brought into contact with urban capitalism in its highly developed form. He acknowledges the power of capitalism. But he questions whether rural societies and cultures are inevitably doomed to disintegrate in its path. He argues forcibly that this disintegration entails both human misery and social disharmony. The political message of the book is that the urban middle class should recognise that its own class self-interest lies in allying with the peasantry to support a smoother rural transition, rather than triumphing in urban growth and rural decline.

In an interview in 1986, he set out his political perspective at this time in more detail:

> The alternative possible development for Thailand is along the line of democratic revolution (*naewthang kan patiwat prachathipatai*)... or it can be called capitalist democracy (*prachathipatai thun niyom*). This is the same direction as Western European countries. I think this is suitable and possible. . . . This will enable everyone in different places in the country to participate in the development of our country. . . . As for the system of economy, it is open to capitalism. This will give opportunities for new development, give opportunities for the bourgeoisie to develop industry as a continuation from the development of trade which has already occurred. We must receive new technologies from the West and benefit from international trade.

Chatthip emphasised that this "capitalist democracy" would be an advance on the "parasitic capitalism" (*thun kafak*) which he describes in *The Thai Village Economy in the Past*. But a few years later, at the time of his review of community culture, Chatthip's expectations of any significant change in capitalism had weakened:

Ideally, the author proposes libertarian socialism. However, in reality, what we face is capitalism. We should therefore have a maximum programme and a minimum programme. The maximum programme is anarchism and the minimum programme is progressive capitalism. In other words, we demand that a progressive middle class share administrative power and the management of the economy with village communities. It must not be a system where the state has extreme power, nor a centralised capitalism where only a handful of capitalists control the economy, or a capitalism that relies on foreigners and exploits the rural people. (138)

Fully half the article reviewing community culture is devoted to a discussion of the fit between the independent, anti-state strain of village culture and the stance of anarchism. He sets out a programme which includes self-reliant local economies, political organisation, and consciousness-raising at the village level, and the transformation of Buddhism from a tool of the state to "an organisation of the people. . . concerned with the real life of the people" (140). However he still believes that "an alliance with the middle class can strengthen the people's movement as a whole" (138), and he wants to "co-opt into the community culture progressive universal elements, such as technology, ideas about efficiency and initiative" from the West (140).

The village culture studies of the mid-1990s amount to deeper case studies of the processes outlined in *The Thai Village Economy in the Past*. The major themes are the same: the persistence of subsistence, the coherence between the local economy and local culture, and the disintegration of the economy in the twentieth century. But the tone has shifted. The intrusions of state and capital to break down the village are portrayed in more aggressive terms. Most of the case studies focus on villages which over the last two decades have fought back against state and capital by shifting to more self-reliant economies, reviving local culture, and building new forms of community organisation. The conclusion of *Watthanatham muban thai* (Thai village culture, 1994) argues that the village community must aim not just to resist, but ultimately to replace the modern state and capitalism.

Over the past twenty years, the rate of change in Thai society has quickened. The supply of land dwindled especially close to urban areas. The resource base of the village community became shaky. Numbers of landless farmers increased. Men, women, and children had to move to work outside the community. Within the community, class division arose and paved the way for disputes. Concern arose within the country that economic change was destroying the village community, destroying the villagers, destroying the culture of the Thai . . .

But the soul of the village still survives, still remains free. . . . This is a distinguishing feature of Thai society, that the soul and ideology of the community still survives.

If the community is to retain its strength in the future, it must expand its network, both in the sense of scope and spread . . . must create an economic system and administrative system which has its foundation in the network of community institutions.

The primary objective is to oppose the power and exploitation of the capitalist system. The next objective is to expand the scope of the community. The final objective is to replace the capitalist system completely. (244–7)

In his political vision, the possibility of a "progressive capitalism" or "alliance with the middle class" had faded into the background. He now sought ways to reduce the role of the state and the domination of capitalism by creating a network of rural communities (*kruakhai chumchon*) which could exist separately, rely on one another, and gradually reduce their relations with state and capital. He explained in interview in 1996:

At the moment I want to support movements and networks which already exist among villages. I would like to help people articulate the system of thought. Researchers and scholars must have a methodology to study histories of village communities, exchange information and experiences, and then give back to villagers their histories and their consciousness. Knowing their own histories will give them strength.

This network building is already occurring among villagers and researchers. I am extending this to Laos. It has to be developed further. Networking is important because it enables communities to survive, to exist independently of the state and of capitalism. Once these networks expand, assist, and reinforce one another, it may reduce the importance of the state and capitalism.

To focus only on resistance to the state or to capitalism is too messy. Villagers need time to find themselves before they can take action.

The people who will sustain this movement are the various local communities. But they must not be led by state nationalism. What is important is a consciousness based on the history of the community. (Interview, 11 October 1996).

Chatthip saw no reason why such networks of local communities should be demarcated by international boundaries. Indeed he now looked to rescue Thailand from parasitic capitalism by borrowing from two very different external sources:

The Thai community culture is durable but it lacks the power to change the community and the society. . . . It is important to accept input from Western culture for progress in material things, science, and technology. But when it comes to mentality, feelings, and ethics, we should draw more from our own local communities and also from Tai communities outside Thailand, which have preserved the character of ancient Tai culture to a great extent in documents, ceremonies, and daily life.[8]

He saw that just as the villages' separate cultural identity was critical to their local strength, so some form of cultural relationship would be needed to bind together supra-local networks. He hoped to find this cultural glue in the common heritage of Tai peasant com-munities throughout the region. The proposal for the cross-border study of Tai communities, written in 1995, includes this passage:

The comparative study of Tai culture has serious implications to the local and national development along the line of "community culture" in Thailand. The social and cultural study of different Tai groups may enable us to find the origin and the root of the ancient Tai. If it was found and revived, it may make clear the consciousness and the uniqueness of the ethnic Tai. It will become a powerful force to gather the strength of all Thai villagers to come together to create and push for a movement aiming to achieve a better life for all. It will be a powerful force because it is bringing the subconscious of the ethnic group to the fore. Interaction with Western culture is significant with respect to material progress in terms of technology and science. But spiritual matters, feelings, and ethical norms are something separate which we have to seek, gather, and recollect from the culture of Tai communities outside Thailand, who still retain the unique characteristics of ancient Tai culture.

Three years later, he restated this perspective even more forcefully:

Village community, folk culture and/or peasant life-way can be the major contributor of "dominant culture" of a nation-state. Tai culture can be treated in that special position, being so identical at both national level and village level . . .

If we consider Thailand as not simply a state, but as a code of Tai culture, this cultural dimension can lead us to effective Thai-Tai economic relations. The implication would be the new perspective of different kinds of political grouping in the future.

Another dimension is the establishment of various kinds of Tai peoples networks, which transcend state boundaries. A political area does not have to mean an expansion of the nation-state power.[9]

In 1997–99, the economic crisis revealed Thailand's underlying reliance on the village economy for food and for the support of the majority of the population. Chatthip urged that this crisis offered an opportunity "to look again at the local peasant community as the basis of the economic life and culture of the people, and to support a new direction in national development, beginning with strengthening from the bottom up, from the level of the family, the local community, and the agrarian economy".[10] In a study on approaches to rural economics, Chatthip and his team noted that the community culture movement had helped to build a new politico-cultural base for rural society but had not provided the economic theory to match. They urged the need to study the real working of Thai peasant economics in detail, rather than assuming this economy worked according to the laws of neo-classical or any other form of (urban) economics. This study should begin from the angle of the peasant and village community, but would have also to include the relations between the rural economy and the other sectors of the national economy. This would lead towards economic planning and growth on a new basis:

> ... each locality has its own life and own cycle of economic reproduction. The local community should have the freedom and ability to plan its own economic development. This may be in the form of a cooperative or other network, with the primary objective of self-sufficiency for community consumption, and a secondary objective of raising the community's productive capacity so that farmers no longer need to over-exploit their own labour. This will enable the community to survive with dignity and future potential.[11]

Chatthip recognises that history itself is a social force. Just as earlier state historians wrote history to legitimise the state, and Marxist historians wrote history to legitimise revolution, Chatthip wants his history to legitimise values found in the village as social forces in the present day. He wants to promote the "good things" about the village community as a basis for further development of a better society. In *The Thai Village Economy in the Past* he hoped this would be possible within the context of the state and capitalism of modern Thailand. After a decade of jolting change which has often emphasised the urban economy and urban values at the expense of rural society, Chatthip's vision of a better society remains unchanged, but his perception of the route towards this society has shifted. Village communities must rely on their own resources, develop their internal capacity, and ally with one another over a broader area to gain the strength to survive and to offer Thailand—and the world—the model of an alternative and better society.

Chris Baker
Pasuk Phongpaichit

## Notes

1. Craig Reynolds and Lysa Hong, "Marxism in Thai Historical Studies," *Journal of Asian Studies* XVIII, 1 (November 1983), 96.

2. Katherine Bowie, "Peasant Perspectives on the Political Economy of the Northern Thai Kingdom of Chiang Mai in the Nineteenth Century: Implications for the Understanding of Peasant Political Expression," Ph.D. dissertation, University of Chicago, 1988; "Unravelling the Myth of the Subsistence Economy: Textile Production in Nineteenth-Century Northern Thailand," *Journal of Asian Studies* 51, 4 (1992); Anan Ganjanaphan has written a review of Chatthip's work, provisionally entitled *Khwam khit lae khwam fai fun khong achan Chatthip nartsupha* [Thought and aspiration of Chatthip Nartsupha] which will appear in the Thailand Research Fund's series on modern Thai thinkers.

3. Atsushi Kitahara, *The Thai Rural Community Reconsidered* (Bangkok: Political Economy Centre, Chulalongkorn University, 1996); Jeremy Kemp, *Seductive Mirage: The Search for the Village Community in Southeast Asia* (Amsterdam: Centre for Asian Studies, 1987).

4. For his recent project on the history of Tai communities outside Thailand, Chatthip selected researchers who are anthropologists, linguists, lawyers, and freelance writers. At the seminar (3 December 1998 in Chula) to review the work, most of the commentators were academic historians. Commentator after commentator stood up and said: this is very interesting but this is not history.

5. "The 'community culture' school of thought," in *Thai Constructions of Knowledge*, eds. Manas Chitkasem and Andrew Turton (London: SOAS, 1991).

6. Chatthip Nartsupha, *Watthanatham thai kap khabuan kan plian plaeng sangkhom* [Thai culture and social change] (Bangkok: Chulalongkorn University, 1991); *Prawatisat watthanatham chumchon lae chonchat thai* [The history of community culture and the Thai nation] (Bangkok: Sangsan, 1997); Chatthip Nartsupha and Phonphilai Loetwicha, *Watthanatham muban thai* [Thai village culture] (Bangkok: Sangsan, 1994) and *Thit thang watthanatham thai* [The direction of Thai culture] (Bangkok: Sangsan, 1996); Chatthip Nartsupha and Phunsak Chanikonpradit, *Sethakit muban phak tai fang tawan ok nai adit* [The village economy of the eastern side of south Thailand in the past] (Bangkok: Sangsan, 1997).

7. The project is reviewed in the special issue of *Tai Culture* 3, 1 (June 1998). The main outputs are in the process of publication.

8. Chatthip and Phonphilai, *Watthanatham muban thai*, 247.

9. "Perspectives on Tai Studies," *Tai Culture* 3, 1 (June 1998), 12.

10. Chatthip Nartsupha, Chinasak Suwan-Achariya, Apichat Thongyou, Voravidh Charoenloet, and Maniemai Thongyou, *Thissadi lae naeokhit sethakit chumchon chaona* [Theories and approaches to the economics of the peasant community] (Bangkok: Vithithat local wisdom series 7, 1998), 272.

11. Chatthip et al., *Thissadi*, 263-4.